ACTA UNIVERSITATIS UPSALIENSIS
Psychologia Religionum
8

E. ANKER NILSEN

Religion
and
Personality Integration

Distributor:
Almqvist & Wiksell International, Stockholm, Sweden

UPPSALA 1980

Published with grant from Swedish Council for
Research in Humanities and Social Sciences

The text has been revised by Phillip Eskridge

© E. Anker Nilsen 1980

ISBN 91-554-0991-1
ISSN 0346-6094

Printed in Sweden
by LITA-tryck, Bjärnum, 1980

Contents

Preface	9

Chapter I
A Theory of Personality Development — 13

Personality integration as a "dynamic field"	15
The two-dimensional dynamic field: The actual life situation	20
The three-dimensional dynamic field: The value system, the ego, and the environment	21
The areas, zones, or fields of integration	24
The factors involved in personality integration	26
1. The value system	26
2. The ego functions	27
3. The actual life situation	29
Our theory compared with Rogers' theory	29

Chapter II
The Value System — 34

The importance of value in psychotherapy	35
Religion and value	38
The need for value systems	43
The development of the value system	45
The hierarchy of the value system	49
The quality of the value system	53
Values operating in personality dynamics	55

Chapter III
The Actual Life Situation — 58

The term "life situation"	58
The objective and the subjective life situation	59
The forming of the life situation	60
The semi-integrated area of the life situation	61
Emotional stability	64
Social adjustment	65

Chapter IV
The Ego Functions — 67

Some philosophical and psychological aspects of the ego functions with special emphasis upon the self-valuing process	68
The self and the ego	69
Self-consciousness	70

Self-centeredness	71
Self-esteem and humility	72
Self-evaluation	73
How self-evaluation is established and promoted	74

Chapter V
Religious experience

Religious experience	75
Definition of religious experience	75
The basic factors in the religious experience	76
Religious crisis experience (conversion)	81
The "God-constructs" in the religious experience of John Wesley	82
The nature of religious conflict	83
Are religious conflicts detrimental	87
Guilt feelings and redemption	89
Neurotic religion	92
Religious experience in growth (sanctification)	95
Growth and faith	98
Growth and love	99

Chapter VI
The Process of Pastoral Counseling

The Process of Pastoral Counseling	100
The need for diagnosis in pastoral counseling	100
The main factors in the integrative process of the individual to be studied	102
The image of God and the actual life situation in the integrative process	103
Self evaluation in the integrative process	109
The encounter with God	111
The basis for encounter with God	112
The experience of sin and shortcomings	114
The experience of forgiveness and reconciliation	115
The experience of confession and absolution	117
Religion in the adjustment to the life situation, the Christian life	117
Levels of integration and healthy tension	121

Chapter VII
The Problem of Values in Psychotherapy

The Problem of Values in Psychotherapy	122
The possibility to introduce values in psychotherapy not violating the scientific base	124
An experiment in treating values in psychotherapy. A diagnostic design	126
The perfectionist neurosis	127
Therapy with problems of values	129
The significance of the therapist's personality in the therapeutic process	132
The therapist's world outlook as a point of reference for the client	135
Research projects and results on the therapist's role in the therapeutic process	137
Conclusions	140

Chapter VIII
Religion, Psycotherapy, and Pastoral Care   143
Religion and psychotherapy   143
The therapeutic process   150
Comparison of psychiatry, psychotherapy, and soul care   152
Religion as a therapeutic agency   155
Religion in the therapeutic process   157
Co-operation between religion and psychotherapy   162

Notes   165

Bibliography   169

Preface

Does religion promote or impede personality integration and development? This is the recurring question which has received greatly differing answers troughout the ages, from the most negative to the most positive. Religion has been, on the one hand, accused of interfering with the growth of personality even to the extent of neuroses and psychoses. Religion is detrimental to the integration of personality. On the other hand, it has been declared that religion is the main factor in the integrating process of personality. It has been stated that man cannot fully be man unless he has religion to some extent.

In our opinion this question cannot be answered with a clear-cut yes or no. Religion is not homogeneous. We have to reckon with different forms of religion. What has been said of one religion cannot be said of other forms of religion. For even though we, as is our task here, are concerned with the Christian religion, we cannot say that throughout the ages and in every place where the Christian religion exists, we are dealing with the same form of this faith. And when we consider the great variety of Christian experience which may be observed in different Christian individuals, we must admit that we have to analyze the varied forms of Christian faith before we can speak of the beneficial or detrimental effects of religion upon the development of personality.

We may say from the start of this inquiry, that not all forms of Christian religion have promoted personality development in a healthy way, and far from all kinds of religious experience have stimulated to personality growth. It will be our task to analyze the quality of these experiences as they promote or impede the growth of personality.

In order to analyze the quality of the religious experience, we must take into consideration the following factors of the growth process: Firstly, the individual's ability to grow depends upon his cognitive opinion of the religious values which operate in his life. In a stricter sense, it is a question of the quality of his image of God as the highest value in his religious system.

Secondly, we have to investigate the individual's experience of his immediate life situation and especially how he perceives his operation in daily life and the relationship between his ideal world of values and the real world of the actual situation in which he finds himself.

Thirdly, we have to take into account the individual's view of himself, whom he thinks he is, his valuation of himself, his opinion of how he acts and works.

The problem which we have to investigate is briefly defined in this way: The religious person feels himself caught in a battle between his ideal world and his real world. The problem is for him to harmonize or integrate these two worlds. In my opinion, the key to understanding this battle lies in the individual's experience of himself and his evaluation of himself, his capacities, his self-understanding and self-acceptance. Briefly stated: We have to deal with three factors which we must analyze in order to find an answer to our problem of personality integration and development: the individual's religious value system, his experience of his actual life situation, and his self-understanding.

When considering the problem of religion's beneficial or detrimental impact upon the integration and development of personality, we are actually dealing with part of a deeper problem, that of the relationship between an individual's value system and his actual life situation. In essence it is a question of loyalties on the one hand and personal needs on the other. This is the old story of the battle between spirit and flesh, to speak in New Testament terms. Psychologically, it is a question of aspiration level and actual performance.

In order to deal with this problem, we have chosen to use different models. First we have our own models which we shall present in chapter I. It will be seen that we use Andreas Angyal's model from his book, "Foundation for a science of personality". His theory is that, in our concern for adjustment to our life-situation (biosphere), we try to combine autonomy (self-government) with heteronomy (governed from outside) and that we never succeed in this effort unless we take into consideration what he calls homonomy (conformity to super-individual wholes). I have also in mind the psychoanalytical model of "superego" "ego" and "id". Our main interest however, is to relate our model of personality integration to Carl R. Rogers' concepts of the individual's "self-concept", "the phenomenological world" and "the fully functioning person".

The background for this book is my M. A. thesis, written for Northwestern University, Evanston, in 1948 on the influence of a person's idea of God upon his self-evaluation, and my Ph.d. thesis on the idea of God and personality integration, written for the same university in 1952. The theory brought forth here has occupied my thoughts for nearly 25 years. What I have experienced in my work as a minister and psychotherapist has substantiated what I then felt was new thinking in this area.

I wish to express my deepest gratitude to my teachers. First of all, to Dr. Carroll A. Wise, professor at Garrett Theological Seminary Evanston. He introduced me to this new trend of thinking and made it possible for me to combine my ministerial work with psychological research and facts. Dr. Anton T. Boisen at Elgin State Hospital gave me the opportunity to practice the new theoretical findings. I feel very much obliged to him. And last but not least, Dr. Carl R. Rogers, whose pioneering work in counseling and psychotherapy has inspired me and rendered meaning to my teaching and writing.

I also want to express my deepest thanks to Acta Universitatis Upsaliensis and the Swedish Council for Research in Humanities and Social Sciences and my friend and colleague, professor Thorvald Källstad, for making the publishing of this manuscript possible.

CHAPTER I

A Theory of Personality Development

Personality development takes place in the same way as the development of all other forms of organic life — through the functions of differentiation and integration. The functions of differentiation and integration are called growth.

Physiology is familiar with this idea. Muscle activities start by differentation of aimless gross movements which characterize the baby's activity and continue in integration of the differentiated movements on ever higher planes. The well differentiated and integrated muscle movements of the artist, the musician, and the athlete, culminate that development.

Psychology traces a parallel process. Emotional life developes according to the same pattern from a more or less diffused feeling of excitement into a more differentiated feeling of specific desires and dislikes. This in time differentiates into the rich and varied emotional life of the adult which in turn integrates into systems of emotions or sentiments. And so it is with the cognitive processes which move from the general to the specific. We have to analyze in detail our ideas in order to put them together into new concepts. Concepts are integrated thoughts.

Personality development takes place along the same lines. This is most easily observed in the ego development. As the ego developes, the child has to differentiate himself from his environment. This first takes place on a physical level as the child learns to distinguish himself from his surroundings, his mother, his clothes, etc. The child continues to integrate his experiences into ever higher systems in order to make successful growth and progress in life.

Gardner Murphy describes three levels of growth: "The growth process necessarily entails three developmental levels: (1) a level of global, undifferentiated mass activity, (2) a level of differentiated parts, each acting more or less autonomously, (3) a level of integrated action based upon interdependence of the parts."[1] This pattern of development may be used for our discussion of the development of personality with special interest in the integrating process.

It seems reasonable to believe that the integrative process follows certain patterns due to inherent dispositions. Biology gives evidence for such structure in the chromozomes and the genes which direct the development of the species. A normal development of each individual of the species follows this pattern. Abnormal development is described by deviations from this normal pattern. The study of the nature of this pattern is still only in the early stages in the biological sciences, and we do not as yet know the complete inner workings of the process. We can only say that it seems reasonable and natural for us to accept this fact.

In psychology we may reckon with the same process in the development of personality even though its analysis is more problematic. Psychology has to reckon with a "steering" factor in the development of the individual. We would like to think that this steering factor (factors) has the same origin as the biological steering factor, and there is no reason for not doing so. However, we have a feeling that this view is not satisfactory when trying to analyze and describe the integrating process taking place in the individual. There seems to be something more than a biological background to the integrative process.

Psychologically, the motivation of these dynamic integrative processes has been perceived and described in different ways. Henry Bergson calls this motivating factor "elan vital" (vital impetus) and from him we have the vitalistic view which emphasizes an inner driving force that directs the individual's growth. Driesch has somewhat the same idea with his term "entelechy" which means activity directed toward a goal. I have a feeling that Adler's finality principle leads in the same direction. Woodworth's "hormic power" and Kurt Lewin's "valences" take the same lead, in my opinion, and even Freud's "libido" has the quality of an "inner driving force".

All these attempts at describing the motivation of the integrative process in personality have one thing in common, in that they lead us beyond the simple stimulus-response pattern of behaviorism. The introduction of the "intervening variables" in the stimulus-response pattern is a step in the right direction. The full step is taken when we admit that personality is a "dynamic organization" to use Andras Angyal's terminology.[2] Personality is in itself the organizing agency, self-aware and self-acting largely through the functions of the ego. This takes place within certain limits, of course, set by the laws of causality, to which the human being has to yield. The human personality is not, however, only a ball tossed around by environmental causes, it is also an actor in the world of finality, busy with integrating, expelling, assimilating in order to obtain goals which have been accepted by the organism.

Scrutinizing this big problem on an operational level, we may say that we have to search for the motivating factor in personality development in the ego function of the individual. I think here we are in line with Freud's concept of the ego functions as the structuring and organizing agency in personality. Ragnar Rommetveit in his "Ego i moderne psykologi" (Ego in Modern Psychology) has the same idea when he states that the ego functions are primarily due to the perceptive and motivating agencies of the ego. Rogers' emphasis upon the self and its symbolizing activity leads to the same goal.

The conclusion must be that the ego functions, in their self-evaluating activity, are at the core of personality development, keeping in mind the "steering" mechanism.

It seems to me that we have not really fully analyzed the motivating factors in personality development before we have taken into consideration the value system of the individual. We have pointed out that the ego functions, especially the self-evaluating process, is of the greatest importance when we are analyzing the integrating process. Our main concern is, however, to relate the function of integration not only to the self-evaluation of the individual, but also to the value system which the individual has created, and which dynamically determines the integrative process going on in the integrative areas of personality.

We believe that the individual's daily life is not only determined by the functions of the ego, but also led by loyalties to super-individual factors. Integration always takes place in relation to something. If this "something", which operates as a leading principle in life, is lacking, it interferes with the integrative process in a detrimental way. Our definition of personality integration is: "Personality integration is the organization of life in relationship to that which man (the individual) considers to be of the highest value to him."

To make it clearer, we may think of this value system in terms of Freud's super-ego, even though we later will explain in more detail in what way we differ from Freud in determining the quality of this value system.

Personality Integration as a "Dynamic Field".
In order to deal operationally with our hypothesis of personality integration it is necessary first to distinguish a "field" or an "area" inside which the integration takes place. We have to make certain assumptions when we start our investigation. Working hypotheses for this study are as follows:

We assume that the integration of personality takes place within a "dynamic field". We are using the term in the same sense as the Gestalt Psychologists do, especially Kurt Lewin's form of the term "field forces". Gardner Murphy and Andras Angyal call it "biosphere", and Carl R. Rogers terms it "phenomenal field" or "experiential field". Adler suggests "life plan" in his purposive psychology. These terms describe the experiences of the organism in dynamic terms showing that something is taking place inside a more or less distinguishable field of experience. This statement means simply that there is something that can be classified as belonging to orderly and meaningful experience promoting growth in the individual.

The process of integration is never to be thought of as static or something which once and for all has been obtained. Personality integration is never to be thought of as a fixed pattern. Integration of personality is a dynamic process.

Personality integration must always be thought of as taking place within certain limits, and in one way or another it is necessary to determine the limits of the integrative process. We need to draw a borderline distinguishing what belongs to the integrated area, and what is not integrated. Within the borders life is meaningfull, coherent. The individual can cope with the problems of life, handle them and solve them in one way or another. He does not get emotionally upset by the probe in this "territory" nor does he get into grave conflicts with his fellow men. Life moves more or les smoothly as long as the individual operates inside this boundary.

The area of integration might be larger or smaller due to the individual's heredity, his physical and mental abilities, his life history, his degree of maturity, etc. Ordinarily, the integrated area can be expected to grow with the age of the individual.

The integrated area varies not only with age, but with the variations in the mental and physical characteristics of the individual. The integrated area diminishes when a person is tired, or he has become sick, or he is under stress in his work or relationships with other individuals. On the other hand, the integration area can be expected to increase on holidays and being in good company. The integrated area then is, as we have seen, not a static area with fixed borders. It is dynamic, always fluctuating.

Outside the integrated area there is a non-integrated zone. Here we find the "material" that has not yet been integrated. It may be integrated as it comes into focus and becomes important to the individual, and calls for attention. It may, however, stay in the non-integrated area as material that has little or no value to the individual. As long as the individual does not pay any attention to it, it does not disturb him. It is outside his concern.

Between the integrated and the non-integrated areas we find an area which we would call the semi-integrated area of personality dynamics. We may also call this area the field in which the integrating (or distintegrating) processes take place. This area is the most important one in the growth process of the individual. This is the area in which non-integrated material becomes integrated as the growth process moves the right way. It is also the field in which integrated material becomes disintegrated when the growth process goes in reverse. This is regression.

The semi-integrated field in personality dynamics is, in one sense, life's own workshop. It is the "greenhouse" in which the life process is ripening. This is the field in which the struggle of life takes place. Here we are facing the threats of life. Here the crisis experiences of life come into focus, some of them leading to victory and an improved attitude toward life, some of them leading to defeat. Peace is not the characteristicum of this area. This is the battlefield in human life. In the integrated area there is peace because of the fact of acceptance and incorporation of reality. In the non-integrated zone there is also peace because what is happening here, if anything is happening, is outside the scope of interest of the individual.

The most outstanding feature of the integrated area is flexibility, that means that operating in this field the individual is at ease and can adjust

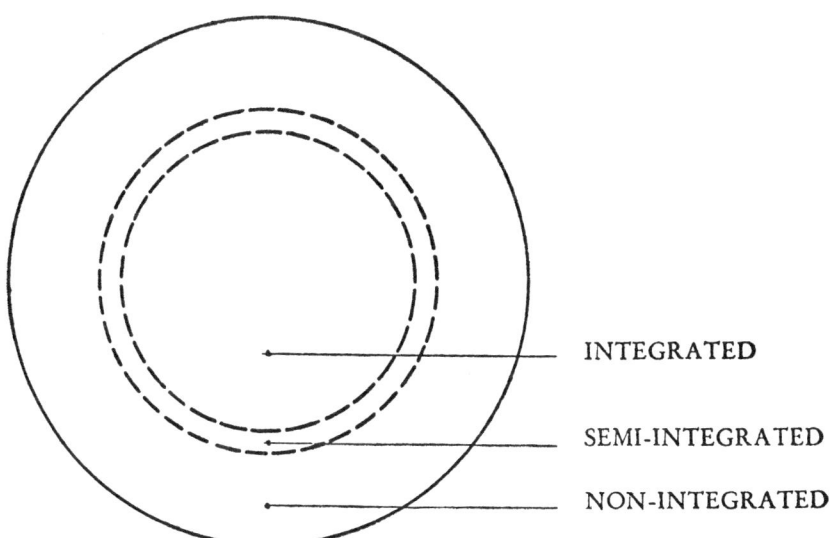

Fig. 1 The dynamic integrated and non-integrated area with the semi-integrated border-area.

to life. The most outstanding symptom of the semi-integrated zone is rigidity, that means that as the individual is operating in this area he feels cramped and unable to make proper adjustments to what he feels is life's stern demands upon him, and he has a feeling of not having resources to meet them. This is the area which "contains" perceived but not integrated material.

We are now ready to study fig. 1, which we hope will be of help in our further analysis.

Before we more fully analyze the diagram, it is necessary to introduce two more terms which we, from time to time, will refer to. One of these is the dimensions of integration. So far we have been speaking of areas and zones, which both refer to the same reality, and we have been speaking of factors operating in the areas and zones. To get a grasp of the inner meaning of the theory which is presented here, it is necessary to speak of the dimensions of integration. By this term, we are thinking of what we already faintly have touched upon when we spoke about the horizontal and the vertical views of the integrative process. Remembering our main interest, namely to investigate the impact of the individual's value system upon his daily living, we can see the importance of discussing these dimensions.

The actual life situation represents the horizontal dimension, including all we have said about the different areas. The horizontal dimension is called a two-dimensional dynamic field. The vertical dimension, which here is also called the three-dimensional dynamic field, represents the individual in his actual life situation in his relation to his value system. (see fig. 2)

And now to the diagram. This diagram is an attempt at clarifying a very intricate psychological process. The diagram represents the individual's experience in the integrative process. And though its representations are far from perfect, it is an attempt at putting, into a visual picture, the experiences of the individual related to the factors involved in the different areas of experience.

At the base of the cone, the horizontal level, we have the individual in his relation to his actual life situation. This means the experience which the individual has in relation to himself and to his environment, his visceral experiences, to use Rogers' terms, as well as his experiences of his world. These experiences are related to the integrating process. He may have a feeling of being "inside" or "outside" the integrated area, or he may have a feeling of operating in the semi-integrated area, where he finds life hard and strenuous, conflict ridden and demanding. He may also have contact with the less interesting peripheral zone, the non-integrated one to which we shall pay very little attention.

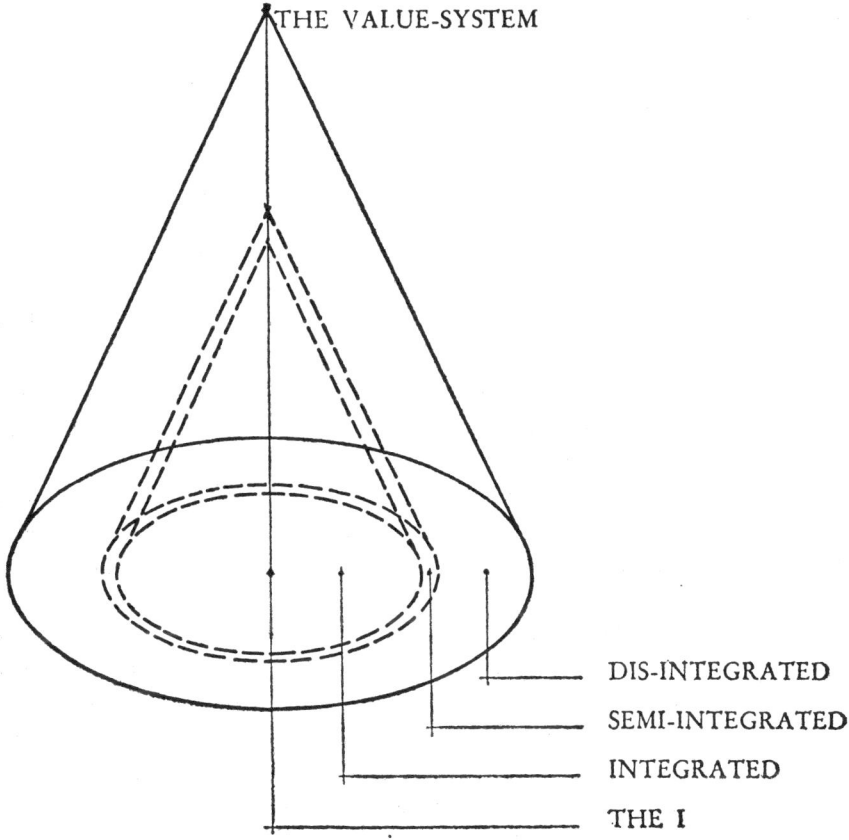

Fig. 2: *A three-dimensional dynamic field of personality-integration: the value-system, the I, and the life-situation.*

The vertical dimension as depicted in the diagram with the top of the cone, shows us the experience of the individual as the value system interferes with the actual life situation of the individual.

The dynamic process which takes place in the semi-integrated zone when the value system interferes with the actual life of the individual, is our concern, especially in its relationship to the integrated part of the experiences.

The process which we have been describing is a process of perception, symbolization and acceptance of new experiences which promote the integration and growth of the individual. Yet at the same time this is the "danger" zone, providing a basis for neurosis and mental disturbances.

We are now in a position where we can analyze in more detail 1) The dimensions of integration, 2) the areas, zones or fields of integration, and 3) the factors involved.

The Two-Dimensional Dynamic Field: The Actual Life Situation

The individual finds himself having experiences all the time. He is steadily shifting in his perceptions and his strivings to make sense out of the manifold experiences he is having. To make sense of ones perceptions, both organic, i.e. visceral perception, and the circumstantial, is what Rogers calls symbolization, we call it, integration.

The individual in his environment, experiencing himself and his fellow men interacting upon him, constitute his actual life situation. It is a dynamic field. This life situation changes from moment to moment, even though it does include some more stable elements. The life situation provided by some vocations may be more clear-cut and steady and for others more vacillating and problematic. Some persons in their occupation generally know what is expected of them, and others never know what to expect the next moment. The first category is represented by the clerk in an office, the farmer on a well-established farm, a railroad official and so on. These people have their day pretty well regulated. They know what to do and when. The second category is represented by persons with great responsibility, whose day is a more changing and flexible one. They never really know what may happen next. The professionals — the doctor, the minister, the diplomat share this characteristic in their work. Responsibility and heavy decisions fall on their shoulders making their day more interesting than, say, the industrial worker, but at the same time more unstable, in that opportunity exists for a steadily changing situation. We know there are individuals who live and work at the limits of their capacities while there are others who live and work in a more routine way very rarely touching the borders of their capacities.

The life situation changes according to status and position, attitudes, feelings, aspirations. It changes also with age. Usually the life situation grows more stable with the years. Older people have a more stable life situation than teenagers.

The life situation is defined as; *all that means something for the individual in his daily living, all that enters into his experience at a given moment*. The most decisive factor in a person's life situation is *himself*, his experiences of his own self, his views of himself and valuation of himself. He is looking at life from his own vantage point. He is always in his experiences. The experiences belong to him, they are his experiences. He can never quit the feeling that his experiences "belong" to him. Estrangement of himself from his experiences is a token of mental disturbance. The individual's perception of himself colours all his perceptions of his world, his environment. It is very important for us to keep this in mind in psychotherapy. The person cannot perceive his world without having, sometimes more in focus and sometimes more in the background of his experience, himself as the "center" of his experience.

The individual also has a feeling that the *environment* belongs to him, his daily work, his family and friends, house and property, all that enter into his experience from this "external" world have relevance and importance for him. He feels that this is his environment, it belongs to him in a special sense, it is a part of him, there is a quality of belongingness in it. But the individual himself is the point of reference in all the events of life. In all the changing experiences from moment to moment the individual experiences himself as the most important factor in whatever happens — he has a feeling that "life-around-me" is a part of "life-within-me".

Correspondence and cooperation take place between a person and the environment in which he feels at home. This correspondence constitutes the experiences of the individual. The study of personality development has always been concerned with this relationship. Social psychology and psychology of personality make this the background for all their investigations.

The life situation is actual and empirical for the individual. He feels life touching him in experiences, impinging upon him always, even subconsciously. Let us call this interaction between the individual and his environment for the *two-dimensional* or *horizontal* life dimension or life situation. It only means that we are viewing the individual in his environment in this way, in order to understand the development that takes place in his personality.

The Three-Dimensional Dynamic Field: The Value System, The Ego Functions, And The Environment.

It may seem unnecessary to introduce a third dimension into a study of personality, the investigation of which is sufficiently complicated without it. All one needs to know about personality, one might object, is to be found in the simple scheme of the individual- environment and the horizontal life situation. The introduction of a third dimension serves no end other than to complicate the whole problem and the methods of investigation. It may also be argued that the introduction of values as a third dimension does not mean a thing, since it can be easily reduced to the two-dimensional field. The values of the individual are introjected from the environment — the values are not outside the two-dimensional field, some contend. Nothing is outside it. By introducing this dimension, we might even be accused of bringing metaphysics into the psychology of personality.

In defence of our inquiry into this dimension, it should be pointed out that in order to understand personality it is necessary to take into consideration the fact that the human being does not exist only in the world of causality. We must concede personality to have at least a small amount of self-determination. It must also be admitted that this self-determination is directed by the goals which he individual sets for his life. Without any discussion of the philosophical and metaphysical background for this statement, we simply state that this can be the experience of every individual, and most individuals think that this is the core of life for them.

The introduction of values as a third dimension in the study of personality is plainly a question of widening the scope of motivation to include leading principles which for the individual's experience are seen as ideals that direct his life. Admitting this, the question is how to handle the problem methodologically. Sooner or later we shall recognize that in order to understand personality development and integration it is our responsibility to inquire into the individual's values — his leading principles, his keenest striving, longings, goals, what he thinks is of value to him, the direction his thinking and work take. What distinguishes man from sub-human beings is the fact, that he can set goals that are over and above the strivings for physical survival.

When we speak of values, it is particularly in terms of moral and religious values and ideals. Psychology of religion has to deal with values. To cut the question of values out of the discussion of religion and ethics is to cut out the vital nerve. The most essential factor in religious life is the values the individual has incorporated into his life. I cannot, however, see that human life as a whole varies any from this statement. Life becomes dull and of little interest if the individual has no feeling of obligation and responsibility toward something that he senses is inspiring him to extend his situation, and no experience of these obligations and responsibilities as something impressed upon him from the outside, something standing over him, having some authority over him. Values act as ideals which, on the one hand, serve as inspiration, and on the other hand, serve as corrections of life and behaviour. Sometimes values interfere with actual life and create conflicts and neurotic behavior. That which acts as ideals in a person's life brings about direction, regulation, and correction or frustration of his entire behavior. It impinges upon his actual life situation, inspiring him, correcting him, maybe condemning him.

It is easily seen that these values are qualitatively different from what we have called the actual life situation. While the ideals are a part of that life situation, they are factors experienced as somewhat outside of our life situation, beckoning us, condemning us or inspiring us. This is the reason why values, as a third dimension in personality integration, should be handled in a study such as this. We cannot see how this value factor can be handled operationally in any other way than as a third dimension, as it qualitatively differs from the actual life situation. Values used in this sense are the most important factors in the integration of personality.

For our purpose, in order to handle the problem, it is therefore necessary to imply a new dimension of life, a third or *vertical* dimension, in addition to the *horizontal* dimension we already have mentioned. The introduction of the vertical dimension in our problem of personality integration makes our project appear more difficult. At the outset it seems unsolvable. This is, however, a pseudo-problem. The question of values and loyalties does not make the problem of personality integration actually more difficult, but even if it did, it should not be ignored, for it is the most crucial factor in the integration of life for everyone. It is impossible to speak of personality integration without bearing in mind that the integration must take place "around or in relationship to something". Values and loyalties are the very core of personality integration. It is in relation to these values and highest loyalties that personality integration takes place, that life at its best develops. Integration on a lower level may take place without much attention to values. One may be integrated on a certain level by saying: "Let us eat, drink, and be merry for tomorrow we die!" That is the "around which" that counts when we are speaking of integration on higher levels.

The introduction of values to psychology is hoped to be a new asset and one which brings hope for new progress. Psychology has not always been concerned with ideals and values. There was a time this area of research was forbidden, its prohibition based upon the assumption that values were not facts, and science is concerned with facts. There is thought to be no bridge between facts and values in science. Science investigates facts, while metaphysics, philosophy and religion supposedly deal with values. This statement rests upon a false assumption, values cannot become facts. The opposite is the truth. As soon as values operate as directing factors in human life, they become facts on line with all other facts with which we are operating in psychology. As such, values are accessible to scientific investigation. Values in themselves are the concern of faith and valuation, as such they are not accessible to scientific investigation, but as soon as values are operating as decisive factors in life they become facts with which science can and must deal. To omit values as operating factors in personality integration from scientific investigation on the basis of their not being factual is to limit the scope of scientific investigation on false premises.

The new trend in psychology is to accept values as operating facts in personality development. As soon as values operate dynamically in the human mind and determine the attitude and behavior of the individual, values are facts. Values are facts as they operate in human life in the same way as all other psychological facts. Values are facts in the life of the individual even more than other facts, they are *the* facts. The most detrimental experience for the healthy integration of personality is the loss of values and loyalties. Changes in the horizontal life situation are not detrimental to the same extent as changes in the vertical life situation, as we shall see later.

The Areas, Zones, or Fields of Integration

It has been pointed out that it is important to think of personality integration in terms of fields inside which integraton and growth takes place. If we look at the diagram (p. 17) we notice that we have distinguished three areas or fields of integration, representing the experiences of the individual in relation to his integration. The individual has a feeling of sometimes operating smoothly, coping with life in an appropriate way. At other times he feels tense and moody, life feels hard and demanding, his possibilities of handling his affairs seem to be reduced, life is working in the wrong direction. Sometimes he has a feeling that life does not affect him att all. He has a feeling of not being interested in what is happening. We have called this first field the integrated field, the second is called the semi-integrated field, and the third is termed the non-integrated field.

We may also say it in this way: In the integrated field we have the material from our experiences, memories, concepts, sentiments etc., symbolized, arranged, systematized, organized. In the semi-integrated field the integrating process is going on. New experiences are sought, symbolized and integrated in the system. The semi-integrated field may also be the "region" in which disintegrative processes are going on. The non-integrated field is the big region outside the immediate concern of the individual.

Inside the integrated area the individual is operating in a free and happy way. He copes with his situation relatively easily. He can handle occurrences of daily living in a smooth, calm and intelligent way. He is the master of the situation. He does not feel disturbed. He has the situation under control.

The border area of semi-integrated experiences, in which integrative or disintegrative processes take place, is the critical area in the dynamic process of personality integration. Operating in this area, the individual has painful experiences, things happen which are disturbing. He does not feel as self-confident as he does within the integrated area. He feels uneasy. He is not quite sure of himself or his abilities. Things may happen over which he has little control. His emotional life is strained. He is keyed up. His muscles are more tense. His brow is wrinkled. He perhaps feels that he can get along, but he has to be very careful. This border area possess many problems for the individual, here is the area of conflict and frustation. In this marginal area just beyond insights and abilities, the individual encounters all kinds of difficulties.

This area is the operational field of those who are dealing professionally with human problems, the psychiatrist, the clinical psychologist, the social worker, the minister. Consequently this area draws our keenest interest in the study of personality.

Thinking of neurosis, we recall what has been said about the semi-integrated area, and discover that the characteristica of neurosis, especially character neurosis and what we would call the "perfectionist" neurosis, are about the same as we have mentioned. The semi-integrated area is determined by anxiety and uneasiness, insufficiency and perplexity. At the same time it is the area in which a solution is searched for in order to cope with life. If we view neurosis in this way, we shall have a more positive way of looking at the problems involved. Neurosis is often thought of as a superficial and wishful solution of life's problems and an accommodation toward life which is not relevant to the real life situation. We think that a more positive view of the mechanisms at work in this region will help us to understand and help our clients in a better way than we usually do. Neurosis is the individual's fight for integration, a new way of coping with life when life has become too troublesome.

The handling of the problems met in this border area depends upon the client, his background, his way of handling his own problems, and the aims and ideals he has set up for his life. At any rate, there are a few lines after which we can observe the reaction of the individual as he is operating in the semi-integrated area: (1) real attempt at facing the problems, efforts to solve them and to adapt to the new situation, (2) aggression, either turned inward against the individual himself with manifestations of self-blame, or open aggression against whomever happens to be on the scene, (3) repression, an attempt to get rid of the problems, (4) postponement, in which the trouble is put off to be taken up for consideration later, or until integration may be arrived at through another solution. In brief, the handling of the problems emerging in the border region of personality integration occurs through acceptance and adaptation, aggression, repression, or sublimation.

The integrative process takes place when the inner area, the integrated area, is widening at the expense of the semi-integrated area, i.e. that material from the semi-integrated area through symbolization and acceptance and structuring becomes part of the integrated area. Personality growth means a widening of the integrated area. The mature personality has a wide integrated area and can stand the pressure of life in a more calm way than the more immature person can. In the maturing process of the individual, it is of importance that the semi-integrated area also is widened at the cost of the non-integrated area. This means more conflict and more pressure but also greater possibilities for growth and development. It is not our concern to keep the individual from facing life in its problems and demands. Our concern is to help people to meet these claims and face them in a right way in order to overcome the difficulties. We shall help the person to grow, and to grow means to face the problems of life and overcome them in order to meet new problems in a more healthy way.

How does it happen that the individual is "pushed" into the area of conflict and growth, the semi-integrated zone? The factors involved are: The value system, the ego functions, and the actual life situation, which we will now discuss.

The Factors Involved In Personality Integration

The integration of personality depends, as we have seen, upon the function of three factors: (1) the value system, (2) the ego functions, and (3) the actual life situation.

1. *The Value System*

The ideals to which the individual gives supreme value dynamically enter into his experience and demand of him the highest loyalty. They are of central importance to his personality integration. The ideals which a person values as important to him form the core around which personality integration takes place.

According to Murphy, the development of the value system takes place through the function of channeling and conditioning, which means that the value system is a heritage of the sociocultural setting in which the person grew up. The value system is, however, woven into the fabric of the person's own strivings, ambitions and longings, his thinking and evaluation. The ideals found in the individual's environment are absorbed by him, and through the process of canalization and conditioning he makes them his own.

The value system serves as the aspiration level in a person's life economy. It encourages his hope, influences his goals, channels his longings and strivings, and helps him determine what, for him, is happiness and disappointment.

The value system gives meaning to life. Even in time of discouragement, bereavement and losses, sickness and death, the value system aids human beings in finding meaning and purpose. Values are facts to be handled scientifically when they enter into the individual's life situation as a dynamic factor determining his life.

2. *The Ego Functions*

The ego functions are at the core of personality. In the terminology of Oates it sounds like this: "One of the focal premisses underlying this whole discussion is that an autonomous self both exists and becomes the stackpole of personality."[3] These functions must be analyzed in order to comprehend personality. Nothing in the science of psychology is as difficult to study as the ego and the ego functions. When experimental psychology started its laboratory work and discredited introspection as a valid method of psychological investigation, the ego and the ego functions were pushed into the back row with little hope of becoming again a real object for scientific psychological research. Psychoanalysis may be an exception to this development. What was gained in perceptional and motivational psychology was lost in ego and personality psychology when introspection was disqualified as a proper method of psychological investigation.

The core of personality is the ego and the ego functions. In order to analyze the personality integration of the individual, these functions have to be keenly analyzed.

Ragnar Rommetveit has made a survey of the ego in modern psychology. We shall use his statements as a basis for our considerations. In his opinion, and he concurs with Allport here, the whole problem of personality integration could not be handled in psychology because of a negative attitude toward ego psychology.[4] The positivistic attitude in academic psychology was the source of this negativism.

The ego is not to be thought of as a thing or substance, but as a motivational system. Ego is a function, not a substance. What are the main functions of the ego? Rommetveit concurs with Anna Freud and Otto Fenichel when he says: "The main ego function is ... a medium, an energy directing, or inner organization that seems to aim at the creation of inner harmony or balance in a chaotic interplay of partly antagonistic impulses."[5]

According to this statement, the ego functions are to be seen as central functions in personality, aiming at integration. Rommetveit also describes the ego as a motivational system which "manifests itself in special impulses to behavior, in will, and in cooperation of, or integration between varied motives."[6]

This recognition of the motivational aspect of the ego functions is a derivative of psychoanalysis. Rommetveit thinks that in addition to this aspect of the ego functions, the perceptional aspect must be added. That is a heritage from social psychology, which includes G.H. Mead's contributions. The matter of perception is bound up with a person's self-concept, how he sees himself. The self-concept is then "a relatively abstract cognitive structure, builtup slowly on the basis of a series of perceptions."[7]

The main ego functions are thus perceptional and motivational in nature. Rommetveit seems to find a synthesis of these two viewpoints in Erik H. Erikson's statement of "ego identity". Erikson says that the most urgent problem for the patient today is what he ought to believe in, who he is or ought to be. He has previously struggled with frustrations that hindered him from becoming what and whom he thought he was. This uncertainty concerning who he really is and what he stands for, which characterizes the patient today, Erikson calls "lack of ego identity".[8]

It can now be seen that the main ego functions are: (1) *self-perception*, (2) *self-motivation*, and (3) a striving for *self-identity*. These functions of the ego come together to form the basis for *self-regard* or *self-evaluation*. The self-evaluation of the individual emerges either in *self-acceptance* or *self-rejection*.

Observing self-evaluation as it functions in the individual's ego is the key to understanding his ego in relation to the development of his personality and personality integration. The self-evaluation, which usually results as an individual compares his actual performances (his life situation) with his ideals (his value system), is crucial to the understanding of the integrative process and the development of personality.

3. *The Actual Life Situation*

Dynamic interchange takes place between the individual and his environment — this is his actual life situation. This is to say that he matures as he perceives and participates in what happens inside him and in his immediate and remote environment, what he is experiencing in relation to the situation in which he finds himself at the moment and what he is experiencing through his imagination and cognitive functions.

What we are concerned with is that part of the environment which interferes with the individual's concerns, that which means something to him, that which he experiences as a part of himself or his world, whether it is integrated in his personality or not. In other words the environment, our fellow men, our work, social relations, hobbies etc., mean something to us as they, through the selective process of perception, come into the focus of our interest and vivify our mental functions, emotionally, cognitively and conatively.

The actual life situation is thus determined as the interaction between the individual and his environment, dealing with the integrative process of this interaction. Our intention in the further study of this process is to see how the individual's valuesystem influences his opinion of himself and how this self-esteem interacts with the individual's operation in his actual life setting. Are his value system and his self-esteem assets in life's struggle or are they detrimental to his way of handling daily living? These are our main questions in this analysis.

Our Theory Compared With Rogers' Theory

Rogers' phenomenological view of the process of personality growth is based upon his analysis of the individual's self-concept and his concept of his world (reality). Diagrammatically he describes these concepts by two excentric circles which somewhat transgress each others limits. Growth is determined by the individual's ability to symbolize his sensory and visceral perceptions of his world in order to have them accepted in accordance with his view of self. Rogers' own statement of this process is as follows: "This theory is basically phenomenological, and relies heavily upon the concept of the self as an explanatory construct. It pictures the end-point of personality development as being a basic congruence between the phenomenal field of experience and the conceptual structure of the self."[9]

It will easily be seen that our theories of personality development are based upon Roger's ideas. It is not necessary for us to analyze the congruence between our thinking and his, it is obvious. We shall only look at the divergences. The locus where our ways differ is on the question of values. My statements here are based upon his writings and personal discussions.

My opinion is that, on the basis of Rogers' thinking, I am taking his ideas a bit further even though I question some of his concepts concerning values.

Rogers thinks that when values come into focus for the child, they are imposed by others and interfere with the symbolizational act of the child. The infant cannot symbolize his experiences, he cannot accept them because of the ambivalence in his feelings, he would follow his needs or instincts but cannot because of values imposed on him by others. This is felt by the child as a threat to the structure of the self. The child's dilemma is, as Rogers states it: "If I admit to awareness the satisfactions of these behaviors and the values I apprehend in these experiences, then this is inconsistent with myself as being loved or lovable".[10] The outcome of this is that the child cannot symbolize his experiences, he has to distort his symbolizational acts, and this in turn interferes with the child's experience of his world. The valuing process has interfered with the child's perceptions of his inner and outer world.

It is clear to me that values may interfere with the integrative process of the child, the claims of parents and important persons regularly run counter to the child's own wishes. It seems, however, to me that Rogers is thinking more negatively of the operation of values than I do. Certainly I agree that in the beginning of personality development Rogers' view is correct, but thinking of further development we must admit that values may operate in the integrative process in a more positive way, i.e., when the individual makes the value system his own. He is overlooking the importance of education, social adaptation and cultural orientation. He is also overlooking the learning process which gives the child an opportunity to establish his own value system as time goes on. I may be wrong, but I have a feeling that Rogers thinks more in biological terms than in social and cultural terms. In my opinion, the self-actualization tendency is not only to be thought of in biological terms. The "overbuilding" made possible through learning, consisting of a set of behavior patterns which are socially and culturally determined, is also part of the phenomenal field of the child. And thus, to accept and be oneself is also to take into consideration this "overbuilding".

We certainly agree with Rogers in his negative emphasis upon introjected values from the environment, but we think that it is necessary to look more positively upon the value system which the individual accepts as his own and which he builds into his own self-structure. We can go even a step further by saying that there are value systems which hitherto have not been accepted by the individual but still influence his personality integration in a positive direction. It is not true that we are always opposed to directives which we do not wholly accept as our own. The reason is that there are certain cultural, social and religious demands upon us which we in our hearts accept as real but in practice do not follow. It is irritating, but it is not disintegrating. We must also be aware of the fact that in the tension between the demands of the value system and our practical living, which often creates conflict, lies the basis for personality integration on ever higher levels.

Rogers goes quite a distance in this direction saying: "Gradually he comes to experience the fact that he is making value judgements, in a way that is new to him, and yet a way that was also known to him in his infancy. Just as the infant places an assured value upon an experience, relying on the evidence of his own senses ... so the client finds that it is his own organism which supplies the evidence upon which value judgments may be made. He discovers that his own senses, his own physiological equipment, can provide the data for making value judgments and for continuously revising them."[11] Rogers thinks that the only way in which cultural values can be accepted by the individual is when they are conceived as giving maintenance, actualization, and enhancement to the organism. "Values are always accepted because they are perceived as principles making for the maintenance, actualization, and enhancement of the organism. It is on that basis that social values are introjected from the culture. In therapy it would seem that the reorganization which takes place is on the basis that those values are retained which are experienced as maintaining or enhancing the organism as distinguished from those which are said by others to be for the good of the organism."[12] This view seems to emphasize a purely egoistic trend in the development of personality and a completely self-centered aim for therapy. In order to escape this fallacy Rogers says that when each individual seeks the enhancement of himself, he will not oppose other people. There are some common trends which will appear when each seeks his own fulfillment. "Since all individuals have basically the same needs, including the need for acceptance by others, it appears that when each individual formulates his own values, in terms of his own direct experience, it is not anarchy which results, but a high degree of commonality and a genuinely socialized system of values."[13] Rogers even states that this is one of the ultimate ends of a hypothesis of confidence in the individual. This statement is in my opinion too optimistic. We cannot see that this view leaves room for the conflicts between individuals and groups which evidently are based upon the strivings of all of them. And what shall we do with the ideological wars between nations in our days?

Let me state very shortly the ways in which I differ from my highly esteemed teacher concerning values. First of all, I think it is necessary to widen the concept of values. The value system must be thought of in a broader sense than we usually do. The value system has to include the individual's life view, his ideals, his morals, and his religion. This means that the value system, even when felt as something that is not yet symbolized in the individual's integrative system, his self-feelings, may act as a directing and guiding factor in personality giving meaning and responsibility to life, sometimes inspiring him and sometimes threatening him. In my opinion the value system, determined as we have done here, is a factor in personality development even when it is not yet wholly understood and symbolized and accepted by the individual. This is the only way in which we can understand the function of religion, and for that matter, all that we call life orientation. And further, the value system is not only operating in the individual's immediate setting as an inner impulse which has to be releaved. It is a question of goals that beckon from afar. The value system is usually a hierarchy of systems, sentiments moulded through the years, builtup in the cultural setting. As such the value system acts as a director of the individual's life, not so much through detailed demands upon everyday living, but rather on the ideals of life stretching out over the long run.

The value system is thus, secondly, ideals more or less accepted, but *still not obtained*. And when it may be obtained, it has a tendency to be pushed further into the future, extended and lifted to ever higher levels. The simple pattern of drive — drive reduction — satisfaction — and quitting the whole thing — does not suit this view of values. The individual has a feeling that the value system belongs to him even when it is not his own i.e. that he has obtained the goal. As soon as he has obtained the goal, the value system fades away. This is the characteristic of the value system in our definition of it, it is a value system that operates in the integrating process of the individual as long as there is some distance between the individual's immediate world of experience and what he thinks life would be like. In this tension integration takes place. When the tension is too high, emotional disturbance is likely to take place, when it is too low, a kind of laissez-faire behavior is likely to appear. When tension is "normal" there is inspiration in the value system that operates upon the individual as a driving force, that he might do his uttermost.

And thirdly, we may think of the ambivalence of the value system. Sometimes the value system operates positively as an inspiration, at other times the value system works negatively as a threat. This depends upon the quality of the value system and upon the possibilities of the individual to meet the demands of his value system.

As a summary we may say that values, according to our definition, refer to what Paul Tillich has called ultimate values of ultimate loyalties, or to use Victor Frankl's terms, the value system of the individual has to do with the meaning of life and responsibility which the person takes upon himself when he has found or thinks he has found the meaning of life. It will be seen that values in our sense do not only refer to the fulfillment of our wishes or desires, but also aims, directives, incentives of our highest obligations. It does not only refer to values created by our inner secretorial system or as a means of keeping our intestinal homeostasis. It does refer to values created by our faith and love. It has something to do with what bishop Eivind Berggrav called "the transgressing tendency".

The question is not whether the locus of evaluation is "inside" or "outside" oneself. The question is of a value system that is "above" ourselves, or if we wish, beneath ourselves, sometimes beckoning us to a better life, and sometimes threatening us because we did not live up to the high ideals we had put before us. It is a question of ideals and ultimate values. We can handle these factors empirically in the integrative process of the individual.

CHAPTER II

The Value System

Values play a greater part in human life than we are ready or able to realize. Our values determine our motives, attitudes, and all our doings. These are questions which people ask: "Is life worth while? Why do I live? What is the purpose of life? How shall I make up my mind in order to choose what seems to be best in the long run?

We think that it is the task of philospy and religion to answer these questions. Psychology and psychotherapy seem to have neglected the fact that values are not "lofty" speculations about the essence of things, but most practical factors in human life, directing our thinking, and feelings, and practical attitudes and performances in life. It is with these functions of values that we are concerned here. To investigate how the value system of a person functions in daily life is a difficult task for psychology. This is the challenge which psychology has to face today. We have been reluctant to take up these intricate problems. We have hidden ourselves behind our quantitative procedures, our statistics, and experiments, and we have told ourselves that the area of values is outside the area of psychology. We have no tools to handle the problems of values. Our experiments have not reached that level of investigation, and our antagonism against the handling of qualitative material has hindered us in opening our eyes to the realities of human life.

The situation seems to have changed. We have begun to realize the significance of widening our scope of investigation. Therapy is one of the main causes of this new concern, as we shall see.

The urge to take up value problems has increased in our time because of the dissolution of moral and religion. Old values in religion and ethics have been replaced by new and poorly tested ones. Often old value systems are taken away before the new ones have taken their place. Maybe we are in that position now.

It is evident that we cannot take up the entire discussion of the value problem. We shall only investigate how the value system operates in the development of personality integration or disintegration.

The problem of value in relation to personality integration has to be scientifically investigated. Robert S. Hartman discusses this procedure saying: "The science of nature measures spatiotemporal being; the science of value measures meaning."[1] He continues saying: "As the natural philosophers developed mathematics as a tool for understanding nature, the moral philosophers are now developing a tool for understanding moral nature. This tool is called *axiology,* from the Greek word *axios,* valuable."[2] Robert Hartman helps us also in stating that we may speak of two kinds of values: factual values, and normative values: "Factual values are observable preferences, appraisals, and desires of concrete people at a given time! Normative values are the ratings... which people ought to give value objects."[3] Further he defines the normative value as a law of nature — idealized, lofty, and universal.[4]

We may stick to the definition of value Henry Margenau provides: A value is the measure of satisfaction of human want."[5] We shall, however, mostly be concerned with the value problem in its normative setting. Then we may say that *value is what the individual rates as ideals that he is seeking to obtain.* As such, values may operate as impulses enhancing the life of the individual or as threats that block the integration of the person.

The Importance of Value in Psychotherapy

Viktor Frankl has perhaps done the most important work in bringing values into consideration in psychotherapy. Frankl has boldly brought out the centrality of values in human life. In an article in the Norwegian magazine Kirke og Kultur (Church and Culture) I have made an attempt to describe the three main phases in the development of psychoanalysis, namely the libidinal (sexual) period, initiated by Freud, the social period, described by Karen Horney, Harry Stack Sullivan, Erich Fromm, Alexander, and others, and then the existential period, developed largely by Viktor Frankl. One might say that the development in psychoanalysis has passed from the biological level through the social to the spiritual (noogene) level.

In emphasizing the need for meaning in life Viktor Frankl has developed his logotherapy or existential analysis, in which he points out that what counts in an individual's life is the values he has the ability to develop and maintain. Frankl sees the "will to meaning" as more important as a motivating factor than the "will to pleasure", which Freud previously put forth, and the "will to power" as Adler mentioned it.

Life without values is life without meaning. It develops what Frankl terms "existential frustration" or "existential vacuum". Whether the values are "creative values", i.e. values which we gain by accomplishing tasks, or they are "experiential values", which means values which the individual achieves by experiencing the Good, the True, and the Beautiful, or they represent "attitudinal values", which are values we obtain by the very attitude with which we face our destined sufferings, they all serve as a basis for the meaning of life.[6] Frankl thinks that "psychotherapy which considers itself to be free of values, is in reality merely blind to values."[7]

Maslow thinks that now is the time to re-evaluate the importance of values in science. After having done with older attempts to answer the question of value, he thinks that the time has come to shape a "scientific ethic", and his opinion is that psychology has the possibility of doing so.[8]

Charlotte Bühler has given due consideration to the value system in psychotherapy. She says that nobody can live without confronting value problems. It is also impossible to undergo psychotherapy without directly or indirectly being involved in these problems. Nor can a therapist devote himself to psychotherapy unless he entertains certain convictions about values in his working with the patients. It is not necessary to present these convictions to the patient. They function, however, as a "background" in the therapist's mind. It is a part of his "reference system". It influences the aims he is putting up for himself in his practice as a therapist as well as the aims he is demonstrating for his patient. They are reflected, consciously or unconsciously in the therapist's questions, expressions, and all his reactions. She also stresses the fact that we can now see that psychologically relevant problems more often are based upon values than on healthy or distorbed projections.[9]

Robert A. Harper states as the main purpose of psychotherapy in his overview of practice in psychotherapy that, "Psychotherapy is, if we may now generalize from our list of common effects, a contemporary means for individuals with poorly functioning value systems to find the support of an apparently strong and successful person in learning a new value system and how to live more effectively thereby."[10]

We shall now turn to the field in which we feel most at home namely client-centered therapy. C. H. Patterson emphasizes that the analyst has the responsibility to assist the client in achieving a more adequate life, not only adjustment to society: "The purpose of this book, then, is to present materials with which to prepare the student to enter into therapeutic relationships with clients. Ethical principles, the place of values in counseling and psychotherapy, and the socio-cultural background of personality development and therapeutic personality change are discussed as the background for counseling relationships."[11]

Rogers says that, "it is very evident that therapy has much to do with what is perceived as "good" or "bad", "right" or "wrong", "satisfying" or "unsatisfying".[12] He admits that this aspect of psychotherapy has been little discussed and so only touched upon from a research point of view. He speaks of the value system as introjected by others from the personal cultural environment. There ensues a period of confusion, Rogers says, when the individual relinquishes the introjected values for his own value judgments. "Gradually", he says, "this confusion is replaced by a dawning realization that the evidence upon which he can base a value judgment is supplied by his own senses, his own experience".[13] In short Rogers states it in this way: "One of the cardinal principles in client-centered therapy is that the individual must be helped to work out his own value system, with a minimal imposition of the value system of the therapist".[14]

In the most recently published book in client-centered therapy, "New Directions in Client-centered Therapy", this statement is made: "Among the schools of thought that make up the therapeutic institution, none have been more concerned with the issue of human values than client-centered therapy".[15] Part Five in this book is dedicated to the problem of values in psychotherapy, which gives us the impression that values are paid an increasing amount of attention. Tomlinson in his paper in the book, argues that "the polemic about efficacy among the various therapies is a product of their differing value systems rather than issues of effect and outcome."[16]

In an article by Rogers, which earlier has been published in The Journal of Abnormal and Social Psychology, he gives a summary of his thinking: "A description is given of the change in the value orientation of the individual from infancy to average adulthood, and from this adult status to a greater degree of psychological maturity attained through psychotherapy or fortunate life circumstances. On the basis of these observations, the theory is advanced that there is an organismic basis for the valuing process within the human individual; that this valuing process is effective to the degree that the individual is open to his experiencing; that in persons relatively open to their experiencing there is an important commonality or universality of value directions; that these directions make for constructive enhancement of the individual and his community, and for the survival and evolution of his species."[17]

Even if we do not fully agree with Rogers in his focussing only upon the "organismic basis" for the valuing process, we think it is necessary to focus on the social and cultural aspects more than he does. There are values which do not stem from this "organismic" basis, but trace their origin back to social and cultural paterns. The dynamic tension between the value system and the actual life situation does not come to the fore in Rogers' system.

Religion and Value

Religion has always dealt with values and ideals. God is usually ascribed the highest value in religion, and an idea of what the individual's life should look like if religiously valid, is always stated. God is, however, the highest value, the supreme value. His word is law. To him the religious individual owes his devotion and service. The concept of God determines to a high degree the life-style of the believer. He will become like his God. His personality integration is dependent upon his view of his God and his demands upon his life.

The main interest I had in studying the problem of personality integration as related to the individual's value system, was to relate the idea of God to his personality development. The following statements are a resumé of the results of these investigations.[18]

The operational definition which we have made use of sounds like this: "The value system is what dynamically makes life meaningful to an individual and directs his important thoughts and actions in life, sometimes inspiring him and sometimes stressing him."

A man's value system acts as a dynamic system of ideals to which he seeks to conform. Quite naturally the concept of God takes a most prominent place in the value system of the religious person. The individual's idea of God determines to a large extent his values in other areas of life. For the devoutly religious person, all other value systems derive their importance and effect from his ideas of God. His moral life, his philosophy of life, his outlook on life as a whole, are derived from his concept of God. Even the lesser concepts of value in his daily life acquire their importance relative to how he perceives his God.

The concept of God which a person carries in his mind is not always a conscious one. Dynamic concepts also operate on a subconscious level. A given concept has been wowen into the pattern of the mind through identification with important persons and because of deep needs.

We are not thinking here of the god-concept primarily in the sense of a rational conception. A person may have a rational idea of God which does not conflict with his other value systems at all. The concept of God he holds may mean something basic to his intellectually held philosophy, but very little to his actual life situation. We are referring to the concept of God in dynamic, not in rational terms. There are individuals who do not have any clear-cut and well defined idea of God, but God as they perceive him has a great influence upon their daily life. We are thinking of the idea of Gud in a dynamic sense, i.e., as a driving force in the individual's life, which molds his life in a certain form and fills it with power and poise, or, maybe, with stumbling blocks and frustrations.

To return to our working hypothesis, the value system of the religious person is mainly concerned with the dynamic concept of his God. That means that it becomes possible to understand the value system of an individual as one comes to grips with his conception of God, granted that his religion means something to him. All other aspects of a religious individual's life will take on meaning relative to this primary underlying fact.

Wading through the great amount of literature on the concept of God, major trends became apparent in the development of the concept of God in history, and in the quality of the concept of God. It was our task to investigate in these rather difficult fields.

In an effort to deal with the concept of God as it operates dynamically in the life of the religious person, let us look at these main tendencies and trends as seen in our Western culture. As far as we can see, through reading the Bible and all the literature we have tried to work through, there are two images of God at extremes of a continuum. On the one hand is God conceived as the mighty ruler, lawgiver, the God of righteousness and punishment. On the other hand he is seen as the God of love and mercy. Using opposite ends of a continuum naturally subjects us to oversimplification of a very complex problem, but in order to deal operationally with the problem, it will be useful. It is not practicable here to study in detail the many possible variations between the two pictures of God. We will stick to authors whom we think are representative of the main trends, or who proceed from our psychological perspective.

Schleiermacher has observed that religion is more concerned with feeling than with reason. The main quality of religious experience is "the feeling of absolute dependence". Analyzing this feeling we shall find that it is ambivalent. On the one hand, there is a feeling of being inferior. On the other hand, there is a feeling of the possibility of getting something out of this position, as he, upon whom I am dependent has the power to help me. This ambivalent feeling comes to the fore when Schleiermacher speaks of feelings of creatureliness. On one hand, there is a man, a creature, kneeling before his creator, acknowledging that he himself is only dust; the creator is omnipotent power. On the other hand, the creature and the creator share similarity in nature, relationship is possible. The God whom the individual feels dependent upon and the dependent creature are related to each other in a kinship which bridges the gulf between them.

This ambivalence, this two-way quality is at the core of religious experience. In the religious experience there must be a more or less conscious concept of God, the mighty creator who authoritatively can do whatever he wishes with his creatures. We are in one sense helpless in his omnipotent hands. On the other hand, God does not take advantage of his power over the work of his hands, as God and men are related to each other in a kinship which gives man courage to draw near to God in spite of everything. Man's creatureliness forces him to bow in reverence and awe before the Almighty, yet man's relatedness to God draws him near to God in love. This two-way quality in the concept of God seems always present in genuine religious experience.

The keenest analysis of this two-way quality in religious experience is found in Rudolf Otto's *The Idea of the Holy*. He perceives the factors involved in the religious feeling as *mysterium tremendum et fascinosum*, an overpowering mystery, yet a fascinating mystery. Otto has described this in a most convincing and eloquent way: "The feeling of it may at times come sweeping like a gentle tide, pervading the mind with a tranquil mood of deepest worship. It may pass over into a more set and lasting attitude of the soul, continuing, as it were, thrillingly vibrant and resonant, until at last it dies away and the soul resumes its 'profane' non-religious mood of everyday experience. It may burst in sudden eruption up from the depths of the soul with spasms and convultions, or lead to strangest excitements, to intoxicated frenzy, to transport, and to ecstasy. It has its wild and demonic forms and can sink to an almost grisly horror and shuddering. It has its crude, barbaric antecedents and early manifestations, and again it may be developed into something beautiful and pure and glorious. It may become the hushed, trembling, and speechless humility of the creature in the presence of whom and what? In the presence of that which is a mystery, inexpressible and above all creatures."[19]

Ambivalence is present in a person's encounter with God — who is at the same time fear-provoking and loving. While one may be frightened and awed, one is also filled with gratitude and assurance. There is attraction toward the *mysterium*, in spite of its awesomeness. Otto finds reference to this ambivalence in the Hebrew word *qadosh*, the Greek word *hagios* and the Latin word *sanctus* and *sacer*, which all have the meaning of *holy*. The meaning of the word *holy* has a double content: (1) it refers to something which is untouchable, distinguished from common life, something that horrifies him who dares to draw near, and on the other hand (2) it is something that fascinates, beckons, attracts, invites. We have difficulties in grasping the total meaning of the word *holy* because common usage has given to it a connotation of *morally good,* which is a later addition to the meaning of this word in the languages which we have referred to.

This double quality Otto calls *the numinous emotion.* He is thus creating a new word in order to get rid of modern references. The numinous feeling embraces both *mysterium tremendum* and *mysterium fascinosum.* Otto is opposed to Schleiermacher's ambivalent feelings of dependence. In his opinion Schleiermacher does not arrive at the special religious feelings by stating that the religious feeling is a "feeling of absolute dependence". Otto says that when Schleiermacher makes a distinction between 'absolute' and 'relative' dependence, reserving the first term for the religious feeling and the second for regular human feelings, he has only made a differentiation of degree rather than of intrinsic quality. Futhermore, Otto feels that Schleiermacher has only captured the religious experience which emphasizes self-consciousness and self-depreciation, not taking into consideration the feelings of elation and fascination which he feels are also part of the encounter.

It is most interesting to note the distinction which Paul Tillich makes when he discusses the application of Rudolf Otto's *mysterium tremendum et fascinosum* to the Lutheran and Calvinistic viewpoints: "The demonic elements in Luther's doctrine of God, his occasional identification of the wrath of God with Satan, the half-divine-half-demonic picture he gives of God's acting in nature and history — all this constitutes the greatness and the danger of Luther's understanding of the holy. The experience he describes certainly is numinous, tremendous, and fascinating, but it is not safeguarded against demonic distortion and against the resurgence of the unclean within the holy.

In Calvin and his followers the opposite trend prevails. Fear of the demonic permeates Calvin's doctrine of the divine holiness. An almost neurotic anxiety about the unclean develops in later Calvinism. The word 'Puritan' is most indicative of this trend. The holy is the clean, cleanliness becomes holiness. This means the end of the numinous character of the holy. The *tremendum* becomes fear of the law and of judgment! The *fascinosum* becomes pride of self-control and repression. Many theological problems and many psychotherapeutic phenomena are rooted in the ambiguity of the contrast between the holy and the unclean."[20]

This is a very sharp and convincing analysis of the *tremendum* as it takes into consideration the horror on one side when an individual encounters the holy even to the point that demonic characteristica are applied to the divine, and on the other side emphasizes the "cleanliness" of the holy. I agree also with his conclusion that the *tremendum* refers to fear of the law, but I cannot agree with his definition of the *fascinosum* as leading to pride of self-control and repression. In my opinion *fascinosum* refers to the feeling the religious person has when he in the middle of horror experience senses the attractive character of God which we generally call *love*. He dares to think that he is loved by God even when he is condemned by him. This is the real ambiguous feeling the religious person experiences as he draws near to God. I especially question his analysis of the Calvinistic tradition. To draw a parallel between *fascinosum* and self-control and repression in this tradition is too rigid. Self-control and repression are not derived from the encounter with the *fascinosum*. It might be the outcome of the encounter with tremendum, here thought of as the fear of the law. Our experience from pastoral counseling and psychotherapy stresses the fact, that when an individual encounters the holy as the great demand upon his life, he has to provide some kind of self-control and very often it leads to repression, or in our terminology to the narrowing of the life-space in order to submit to the demand.

William James has observed the ambivalence of religious feelings and describes a difference between "the once-born" and "the twice-born", between the "healthy" and the "sick" soul. Originally it was Francis W. Newman who described "the once-born" and "the twice-born". Here is his description of "the once-born": "They see God, not as a strict Judge, not as a glorious potentate but as the animating Spirit of a beautiful harmonious world. He is benificent and kind, merciful and pure. This type of religious person generally has no metaphysical tendencies, he does not introspect, hence is is not distressed by his own imperfections. Yet it would not be correct to call him self-righteous, for he hardly thinks of himself at all. This childlike quality of his nature makes religion very happy to him. He, as a child before an emperor in whose presence his parents tremble, does not shrink from God. He is not perturbed by any of the qualities of the severe Majesty-God. He perceives God's character, not in the disordered world of man, but in the harmony and order of nature. He perhaps sees a little sin in himself and in the world and human suffering which leads him to tenderness. Thus, when he approaches God, no inward disturbance occours, and without being quite 'spiritual' he has though a certain complacency and romantic sense of excitement in his simple worship."[21]

In contrast to this William James speaks of "the sick soul", which is a correlate to the "twice-born" man. The sick soul emphasizes the demands of God upon his life. He sees more evil in the world than good. He is painfully aware of his sins and misfortunes. Sin is not to him something that is commited now and then because of misunderstandings. Rather, sin is embodied in the very nature of the human being. The sick soul needs reconciliation with God. He needs atonement and forgiveness. He must be converted, receiving a new spirit.

Here we observe two disparate concepts of God and the human response to them, two perceptions of God functioning in the religious mind with effects leading in opposite directions.

This short survey provides background for our hypothesis that God in the Hebrew-Christian religion both is conceived as the frigthening God of justice exerting his wrath upon human beings and as a merciful Father of love and grace, and that the concept of God in these traditions exerts a great influence upon the religious experience, which in turn affects the integration of personality, in the first place as an impediment and in the second place as a fascilitator of the integration. We have chosen to term the concept of God in the former instance "The God of Law" (Deus Legis) and in the latter, "The God of Love" (Deus Caritatis)

It is outside the scope of this book to go into detail, knowing that these two concepts of God run throughout the Bible and they are the basis for discussions and disputes all through the history of the church. The turning points in the history of the church have always been associated with a shifting in the emphasis upon the concept of God. Here we shall leave it for the study of the patient reader to read my doctoral dissertation on "The Idea of God and Personality Integration".

The Need for Value Systems

One of the most important aspects of human life is that the individual creates for himself a value system to which he has a feeling of obligation. He has to arrange his likes and dislikes according to his value system, and he has to analyze and register his needs and their gratification in relation to the system. He has to build up a hierarchy of need-fulfillments which in turn determines his motivation.

This structuring of interests is a part of the ego-functions which we shall analyze in a following chapter. The main function of the ego is to structure the chaotic id-impulses with the superego-ideals.

In order to function in life, the individual must develope value systems which on the one hand inspire him to go forward or on the other hand threaten him. This is his obligation because he has no overview of all his needs and the manifold ways in which they are satisfied, and it is necessary because the shortage of time does not allow him to fulfill all his needs, and he has no possibility or power to meet all his needs in the time space he has at his disposal.

The benevolence of the value system is easily seen in the integrative process of the individual. The value system serves as an economical agent saving power for the most important activities and as a structuring agent in so far as it gives harmony to the different activities and peace of mind as it serves as a regulator of behavior.

On the other hand the value system may interfere with the integration of personality. In my opinion, this is to be seen in three areas. First, when the obligations laid upon the individual from his value system are too rigid and demanding. Second, when there are interfering and combatting factors in the system, and thirdly, when the value system is too weak and too loosely knit together, lacking the power to keep the interest of the individual.

The great Norwegion dramatist, Henrik Ibsen, has demonstrated all these three trends in his dramas. "Brand" is the exemplification of the person who has a strong and demanding value system, which leads him to overemphasize the demands upon his and other people's lives to the extent that he kills his wife and at last himself when the glacier tumbles down from the mountain, burying him in cascades of snow and ice, and he hears a voice saying:

"Here it is not a question of the human will's quantum satis. God is Deus Caritatis."

On the other hand Ibsen let "Peer Gynt" stand for the person with too low a value system. He does whatever comes to his mind, and is living in the world of fantasies. And the outcome is very poor. The button-moulder can make no button out of Peer. There is no material for such moulding. And the characteristic situation for Peer is when he is sitting at the end of his life peeling an onion saying: "Blade after blade, and nothing more than blades, and no kernel". In "The Wild-duck" Ibsen is demonstrating combatting value systems, one system which has connection with the "real" world, and the other dominated by fantasies and dreams. The end of the story is a shot in the loft-room that kills Hedvig the symbol of combatting value systems.

When the value system has to be revised and reorganized it gives rise to severe conflicts. When the value system becomes disorganized, or part of it does not work and a new value system or systems are not available, it means severe mental disturbances for the individual. It might even lead to the abandoning of the value system or lowering of the ideals below that which the individual feels is necessary to keep up a somewhat reasonable self-respect.

We may say that, on the one hand, the loss or change of value systems may lead to conflict which may provide a basis for new and better value systems. On the other hand, this may lead to neurosis and mental illness, or to a laissez-faire-life-style.

The Development of The Value System

Every normal individual will in the course of life establish his own subjective value system, which will either inspire or condemn him. As soon as the human being confronts his social and cultural environment, he is met by rules and conventions which he's supposed to yield to in order to be accepted. Simple things as how to eat, dress and behave in daily situations, are governed by the value system which is accepted by the individual's environment, his parents and peers. Value systems are put before the child in his home. In school he has the same experience. Everywhere, he finds himself submitted to laws and regulations which are based upon certain accepted values.

The formation of the value system is, first of all, an outcome of the cultural and social setting in which the individuals grows up. He tends to take over the value system of his own cultural and social setting, especially from parents, school, church, and playmates.

The development of the individual's value system comes through identification with persons who are important to him. He takes on the value systems of important people in his life through introjection and identification. As the superego is builtup in the individual in this way, the value system comes into being.

Even if these environmental factors are the most outstanding, they are not the only ones which aid in the formulation of the individual's value system. The individual has his own selective capacity, determined partly by his intellectual ability, to observe and assimilate, to accept or reject, to distinguish the important from the less important, and further depending upon the individual's emotional life which colors the emphasis he lays upon different values. The conflict between the socially and culturally imposed value systems and the value system which the individual himself creates is one of the severest conflicts in life. The integration of personality depends to a large extent upon how an individual can clear up this conflict.

Rogers has a very interesting view of the development of the value system. He states that the infant at the outset has a clear approach to values. He prefers those experiences which maintain, enhance, or actualize his organism, and rejects those which do not serve his end.[22] The value system is flexible and the child has the locus of evaluation in himself.

Development in the valuing process is characterized by the introjection of other people's value systems in order to gain or hold their love, approval and esteem. Then the youngster relinquishes the locus of evaluation which was his in infancy, and places it on others, the result of which is rigidity in relation to the value system. He has to stick to it. He is unable to change it. "I believe," he says, "that this (rigid) picture of the individual, with values mostly introjected, held as fixed concepts, rarely examined or tested, is the picture of most of us."[23] And further: "... we have divorced ourselves, and this accounts for much of modern strain and insecurity."[24] He continues: "This fundamental discrepancy between the individual's concept and what he is actually experiencing between the intellectual structure of his values and the valuing process going on unrecognized within — this is a part of the fundamental estrangement of modern man from himself."[25]

"This tension is released in therapy when the client's experiencing becomes more and more open to him, as he is able to live more freely in the process of his feelings, then significant changes begin to occur in his approach to value. It begins to assume many of the characteristics it had in infancy."[26]

In my opinion this is a limitation of the valuating process in the individual, even if I fully agree that this viewpoint is of the greatest importance in order to reach an understanding of the implication of the value system upon the individual's behavior. It seems to me that Rogers thinks more in terms of regression than in terms of development and integration of personality. In order to be fair to my great teacher, I will admit that Rogers also says that the mature person does not only go back to infancy in order to get along with his values. The maturing process is in one way different from the child's relation to his values. The difference consists of the fact that the mature person's values are more fluid and flexible and more differentiated, the locus of evaluation is established firmly within the person.

Still I have the feeling that something is missing in Rogers' viewpoints on this matter. He does not give due attention to the fact that even when the locus of valuation is inside the person himself, there are values that the individual has accepted but not obtained, values that serve as ideals which are not forced upon the individual but accepted as leading motives. How these values, which primarily are established and formed by the socio-cultural setting but gradually accepted by the individual, are integrated in the individual's life, is our main concern. When Rogers says that there are no longer any universal values "out there", but universal human value directions emerging from the experience of the human organism, then I think this is a one-way view which cannot be true. He feels that the reason he can say so is because: "I hypothesize that it is *characteristic* for the human organism to prefer such actualizing and socialized goals when he is exposed to a growth promoting climate."[27]

As we have seen, Rogers thinks of values more in terms of an interfering factor in the growth of the young child. We think more in terms of values as an integrating factor in the growth experience of the child. If the values of the parent are demonstrated to the child with love and understanding and the child can have what Erikson calls "basic trust", then it means that the child may experience meaning and safety in the presentation of values. The child has to accommodate to the social environment. If the child feels this environment is hostile, I can understand Rogers' position. If the child's environment is conceived as friendly and helpful, I cannot see the dangers that Rogers is demonstrating.

Maybe we can come to grips with the problem when we anew state our main position on this problem of values. It is convenient for us to think of values at least in two categories. First, we look at values from the basis of need, physical or mental. Values are then defined as whatever that can satisfy the need. On the other hand, we will think of values in terms of something we put up as ideals or goals for our life, something that is worth while from the standpoint of the cultural setting in which the individual lives and which he embraces as valuable socially, culturally and religiously. We can also say that values in the first sense, are mainly biologically based, and in the other are culturally based. Bühler speaks, as we have seen, of factual values and normative values.[28] She speaks also of values that serve human need, and values that have their origin in norms which often are in contrast to the need-regulated values, and she adds to these the cultural values which do not have their origin either in personal need or in any moral codex. She speaks also of factual and potential values. A little bit oversimplified, we may say that she is talking about two different kinds of values, one more need-regulated and one more goal-directed. It seems to me that Charlotte Bühler mainly has in mind the goal-directed values. She even defines value in this sense saying that, "Values are preferred goals"[29] Her interest seems to be to discover how these goal-directed values are established and formed in the little child. She arrives at the same conclusion as Erikson, saying that the answer is to be found in the process of identification and the development of social roles. Charlotte Bühler sees the development of the value system in relation to the development of the self. In the child's activity and selectivity, in the ability to imitate and identify, lies the basis for the development of the value system. And she feels, as does Erikson, that the real basis is to be found in the ability of the child to experience "basic trust". This basic trust creates a fundamental "faith" through which the healthy child confronts the word. And this faith creates expectation of love and care from those who are close to him, which in turn gives the child opportunities to be active in a world which is experienced as his own.

Erik H. Erikson refers the building of the value system to the process of identification.[30] This process, he says, is a process which takes place in *the individual's deepest inner life* but at the same time in *the center of the culture of his group,* a process which at its basis determines these two identities identity.

Erikson speaks of different kinds of identity, ego-identity, individual identity, and cultural identity. This last identity, the cultural, he describes as an ego-synthesis, an internal solidarity with the ideals and identity of a group and a worldwide general identity.[31]

The problem of identification in Erikson's view, is a question of a sociocultural process. In relation to the standards, the ideas, and the ideals of the child's cultural environment, he is able to develop his own identity. Erikson thinks that the greatest mistake of psychoanalysis is that this function has been overlooked. The development of the individual's identity is a reciprocal action between the growth of the ego-functions of the individual and his feeling of obligation to standards set before him by his cultural environment. On one side there are the demands of the cultural setting, on the other side there is a growing experience of the self and its demand for self-realization. Erikson refers here to what he calls the epigenesis of personality, which means that the growth of personality follows a general law, namely that all that grows has a basic plan and that in its personal experiences, provided that the child has received a fair amount of good guidance, follows the inner laws of development that provide a series of opportunities for meaningful cooperation with those persons who care for the child and even the institutions that stand ready for the child. We might say that Erikson's conception is that personality develops step by step according to the pattern that is inherent and predetermined in the human organism's readiness to be driven to and to be conscious of and be able to cooperate with a larger and larger circle of relevant individuals and institutions.

In Erikson's view, there is a cooperation between the "organismic" development and the demands of the culture, which in my opinion gives a more adequate picture of the real situation. My experience in therapy leads in the same direction, and it gives me an opportunity to follow up my ideas concerning the beneficial influences of the value system on the integration of personality, even though I have my eyes open to the fact that the value system may interfere with the integration and even be detrimental to the growth of the individual.

Erikson sees in the crisis of young people in our culture, a search for identification which mainly expresses itself in the search for something in which to have faith, people or ideas to believe in. He says that "the social institution that is the guardian of identity is just what we call ideology".

It seems convenient in order to deal honestly with the problem of values, to consider values in a broader sense than is represented by motivational and operational psychologists reducing values to a question of need-fulfillment. Values serve, even from a very early stage in the development of the human being, as ideals and goals which either serve as beacon lights leading the individual on his way to integration or interfere with this process when the ideals are too ambitious.

The Hierarchy of the Value System

So far we have been discussing values in terms of need-satisfying agents or goal-setting agents. Even when Maslow defines a value as "the measure of satisfaction of human want,[32] he distinguishes between 1) expressive behavior, which is a functional striving — we do as we do because we are what we are, and 2) coping behavior which is purposive goal setting behavior. It is evident that we cannot speak of values in other aspects than in relation to need and want. Even the goal-setting value system is based upon human wants, want of something to long and work for. It seems right, in order to come to grips with the value system or systems, to base our investigation on the motivational aspects in psychology, especially when we try to analyze the hierarchy of the system. This view is clearly also Maslow's, as he discusses the means and ends of motivation: "It is characteristic of this deeper analysis that it will always lead ultimately to certain goals or needs behind which we cannot go, that is, to certain need-satisfaction that seem to be the ends in themselves and seem not to need any further justification or demonstration. These needs have the particular quality in the average person of not being seen directly very often but of being more often a kind of conceptual derivation from the multiplicity of specific conscious desires. In other words then, the study of motivation must be in a part the study of the ultimate human goals or desires or needs."[33]

We shall follow the steps of Maslow's hierarchy of basic needs, keeping in mind that he defines value as "the measure of satisfaction of human want", and also keeping in mind that the "higher" needs can only be met as the "lower" needs are satisfied.

Maslow starts with what he calls *"basic needs"*. He discusses here the physiological needs. He opposes the old homeostasis concept and he cannot accept the concept of appetites either, and he also opposes the tendency to compare human needs with, for example, the needs of rats.

He goes on analyzing the *safety* needs which come to the fore when physiological needs are satisfied.

Then come the need for *belongingness and love.* "In our society the thwarting of these needs is the most commonly found core in cases of maladjustment and more severe psychopathology".[34]

The esteem needs he defines, on the one hand, as the desire for strength, for achievement, for adequacy, for mastery and competence, for confidence in the face of the world, and for independence and freedom. On the other hand, it stands for the desire for reputation and prestige, status, dominance, recognition, attention, importance, or appreciation. He says that "An appreciation of the necessity of basic self-confidence and an understanding of how helpless people are without it can be easily gained from a study of traumatic neurosis."[35]

Then comes Maslow's most important need, as I understand him, *The need for self-actualization.* He feels that what a man *can* be he *must* be. It is interesting to compare Maslow's need for self-actualization with Kurt Goldstein's need for self-fulfillment and Carl Rogers' term that the most important thing for the individual is "to become what he is", to fulfill his innermost intentions.

The desire to know and to understand, implies the desire to know and be understood, the desire to satisfy curiosity, to know, to explain and to understand. And finally we come to the *aesthetic needs* on which there has been very little research.

These are the seven basic needs which, according to Maslow, aim at the related values, and to which I have no objection. I have read that Maslow has mentioned still another need, the *need for a personal reference system, a philosophy of life.*[36]

On the basis of these Maslowian needs, we may have the courage to create a hierarchical value system with great flexibility and variation for individual preferences. At the base line we have values that may satisfy physiological needs such as food, water, air, sexual partner, etc. At the next stage we may speak of values that can satisfy the need for safety; house and shelter, companionship, friends, guns and amunition, etc. The third stage may be signified by values that fill the need for belongingness and love, as parents and spouse, society and group, etc. The fourth stage may be standardized as the fulfillment of the esteem needs, which would mean values such as grades at school, diplomas, token of honour, friends in high position, symbols of prestige and status, etc. On the fifth level we find values such as work, especially creative work, hobbies, etc. On the sixth level the values must be books and laboratories and schools and universities. The seventh stratum has values such as art, nature, waterfalls and sunshine, and the smile on the face of a beautiful woman. If we may include an eight level, the level of personal reference and life-view, the values are the personal history of the individual, his memories, a trend in philosophy or a philosopher, a moral codex, religion, and so on.

We do not think that all authors will agree with us in our statements here. Maybe we have left out vital values in life, and maybe we have overemphasized some and minimized others. As we go through the list we will quote some authors especially focussing on what the authors think of the supreme value, or the top of the hierarchical pyramid. Maslow feels, as we have seen, that the supreme value is that which satisfies the individual in his search for self-realization. He says that "... it looks like as if *there were* a single ultimate value for mankind, a far goal toward which all men strive"[37] Futher, he states that this may be expressed by various terms, and he mentions: self-actualization, self-realization, integration, psychological health, individuation, autonomy, creativity, productivity, etc. Maslow thinks that self-actualization is, by far, the one and ultimate value in life. He explains self-actualization in this way: "That is to say, the human being has within him pressure (among other pressures) toward unity of personality, toward spontaneous expressiveness, toward full individuality and identity, toward seeing the truth rather than being blind, toward being creative, toward being good, and a lot else, That is, the human being is so constructed that he presses toward fuller and fuller being and this means pressing toward what most people would call good values, toward serenity, kindness, courage, knowledge, honesty, love, unselfishness, and goodness."

For our special interest, it is convenient to note that Maslow sees in the religious field the fulfillment of the need for self-realization, which here is seen as the transcendence of self, the fusion of the true, the good and the beautiful, contribution to others, wisdom, honesty and naturalness, the trancendence of selfish and personal motivations, the giving up of "lower" desires in favor of higher ones, the easy differentiation between ends (tranquility, serenity, peace) and means (money, power, status) the decrease of hostility, cruelty and destructiveness and the increase of friendliness, gentleness and kindness, etc.³⁸ Even if this characteristic of the function of religion in giving the individual the opportunity to express himself and be himself, is, perhaps, a little too optimistic, not taking into consideration that religion also can function in other ways negatively, as we will mention, we enrole this statement with great satisfaction. Maslow is not only in harmony with the best in religion, he is also in harmony with the best in the ancient greek philosophical tradition where the supreme value is: truth, goodness, and beauty.

Erich Fromm thinks in terms of love when he presents his conception of the supreme value. His view of values is very interesting: "The thesis is that *values are rooted in the very conditions of human existence; hence that our knowledge of these conditions, that is, of the "human situation", leads us to establishing values which have objective validity*; this validity exists, only with regard to the existence of man; outside of him there are no values".³⁹ He continues to say that "There is only one passion which satisfies man's need to unite himself with the world and to acquire at the same time a sense of integrity and individuality, and this is *love. Love is union* with somebody, or something, outside oneself, under the condition of retaining the separateness and integrity of one's own self."⁴⁰ And he concludes by saying: "Indeed, out of the very polarity between separateness and union, love is born and reborn."⁴¹

Kurt Goldstein has much the same opinion, referring to the importance of the value system, and a definite value for the creation of mental health in the individual. He also thinks that "... value ... is a judgment determined by outside factors, by religious, metaphysical, scientific, or social convictions."⁴² The need for a definite value in therapy he states like this: "Anticipating my results, I came through the observation and treatment of sick people, to the conclusion that the behavior of patients could be understood only if it is considered as determined by a *definite value* and that *we can help the patient only when we take account of this value.*"⁴³

Walter A. Weiskopf mentions, that in his opinion there are three different approaches to values in modern thought: 1) The naturalistic approach. The facts are here given through our senses. 2) The humanist approach. It takes into account the totality of human experience, including not only the facts of the sensory order, but the inner experiences, the results of imagination, fantasy and thought. It is an attempt to grasp the total human situation with "its transcendence, consciousness, self-awareness, and freedom". 3) The ontological approach seeks to transcend the facts of sensory observation (naturalistic) and of intuitive experience (humanistic). "It derives its image of man from the analysis of being as such and of the place of human existence in the totality of being."[44] This last point is in accordance with Paul Tillich's view and with him the existentialistic vew: "Value is man's essential being, but as an imperative against him".[45]

In my opinion, Andreas Angyal has given one of the best schemes of the hierarchy of values, stating that we may speak of 1) autonomy, which means life governed by oneself, 2) heteronomy, which is life lead from the outside, and 3) homonomy, which means conformity to superindividual wholes. In his own words: "For this principle we propose the term *"trend toward homonomy,"* that is, a trend to be in harmony with superindividual units, the social group, nature, God, ethical world order, or whatever the person's formulation of it may be."[46]

From this discussion we may extract the following facts: 1) In a hierarchy of values we have to reckon not only with values set by physical and actual tensions and situations but also with values emerging from the individual's personal references and cultural norms and settings. 2) Discussing the hierarchy of values, we cannot escape the formulation of the supreme value (values). It seems evident that Angyal is right when he states that this is a trend in the seeking for personality integration. 3) If we are seeking this supreme value, we regularly have to seek outside ourselves. 4) This supreme value takes on the character of a goal, an end, an ideal, which though we've not yet obtained, are seeking, longing, and sacrificing for.

The Quality of the value system

A more specific definition of the value system takes into account the quality of the value system, what kind of values we are speaking about. We may speak of religious value systems. In our opinion there are more religious aspects in the individual's value system than we at first will admit. Only to speak of the supreme value has something of the religious aspect to it. But a person's value system need not be religious. In any case we must admit that some form of philosophy enters into the value system. This we will call the individual's philosophy of life, which may be based upon a more or less fundamental philosophic system, or a more private view of life which the individual has arrived at through the systematization of his experiences. It seems to me that modern man bases his value system on empirical-materialistic facts, referring more and more to the facts of science. Modern Western society is on its way toward developing such a value system in our time, a system in which religion seems to be outdated.

The reaction to this development is that we form more and more quasi-religious value systems. Some sort of religion must enter into the value system of a human being.

There are two major qualifications of the value system, which will be of the greatest importance for our further discussions and at the same time fully related to what we have demonstrated up to now. The first is the fact that a value system may be imposed upon the individual or it may be accepted by the individual as a part of his own orientation in life. The quality of the "ownership" of the system is the most important aspect, a feeling of having accepted the value system, even if the locus of evaluation is not only within oneself. The feeling of the value system being accepted and made a part of one's own personality even when it functions as a goal not yet obtained, is the mark of a healthy value system. Secondly, we have to pay attention as to whether the value system is fixed or flexible in order to operate smoothly in the life situation in which the individual finds himself in a steadily changing world.

Rogers thinks that the development of behavior disorder depends upon a fundamental conflict between the individual's evaluational thoughts based on sensory, visceral, and affective responses, on one side, and on the other, the evaluative thoughts of others. He believes that behavior guided by the "values of others" may lead to disorder, while behavior guided by the "one's own values" will never lead to disorder.[47] We agree with this statement. We cannot, however, see that the starting point for the evaluative process is always based on sensory, visceral, and affective responses. This process may have cultural and social, ethical and religious origins also. The sum total of the experience of the society in which the individual is living, is, in many ways, codified, and the individual has to deal with it in some way. He may ignore it, and take the consequences of his behavior. He may unwillingly submit to it. And he may discover the benefits of the codes and rules, accept them and integrate them.

The great question is not from where the value system has its origins. The question is how it works, whether it is as an alien system which intrudes upon the individual's integrity, or whether it serves as a goal for his aspirations, accepted as a part of his world-view. It is the non-accepted value system, imposed by others, which is detrimental to the individual, even when it has the confirmation of society. The non-accepted value system interferes, as we shall see, with the individual's self-esteem and makes him inferior in his life and work.

The flexibiliy of the value system is of the greatest importance for the integration of personality. We usually think of the value system as a fixed system. We do not think so much of changing the value system as we think of changing life-style so that living may accommodate the value system. However, the opposite must be the case fairly often during a person's lifetime.

In religious life the fixation of value systems is very clearly seen. In the Christian Church we have quite a lot of dogma, which is the sum of the experience of the church moving through time and history. This sum of previous generations' insight should be the directing aims of the believers, helping them to grasp the life which the church stands for. Very often these dogmas have become strict conventions to which the believer has to pay all his respect and attention. If not, he is condemned to the uttermost darkness. This is in contrast to the great founder of the Christian religion, Jesus Christ, who said: "Ye have heard that it was said by them of the old time . . . but I say unto you."[48] His religion was a religion of the heart, and the willingness to follow by free enterprise and free will, in opposition to the value system of the old times. His marvelous new orientation was in the direction of the full and free acceptance of the values he demonstrated.

What is easily seen in religion is not as easy to discover in other areas of life where values play an important part. I will, however, insist upon the fact that we all have our dogmas, which very often are more fixed than any religious system could conceive.

The value system must be flexible if it shall serve the ever changing life-situation in which we have to live. The value system must serve life, or as Jesus put it: "The sabbath was made for man, and not man for the sabbath."[49] But even when we agree on the flexibility of the value system, there are some basic values which cannot be questioned, such as honesty, truth, beauty, good will, etc. Maslow feels that it will be possible to shape a "scientific ethic" which will take care of this important task for the human being, and he has no doubt when he states that psychology has the possibility of doing so.

Values Operating in Personality Dynamics

Our hypothesis is that the value system of the individual is a deciding factor in personality structure and dynamics.

Carl Rogers is open to the significance of values in psychotherapy even when he states that it is not the job of the therapist to induce his value system on his client. He says: "In these days most psychologists regard it as an insult if they are accused of thinking philosophical thoughts. I do not share this reaction."[50] Rogers refers to Kierkegaard in his chapter on "To be that self which one truly is" saying that the counselor has to answer the question raised by the client: "What is my goal in life? What am I striving for?" Rogers does not think in the same terms as Kierkegaard, who is thinking in terms of glorifying God and preparation for eternity. Rogers follows Maslow, saying that self-direction, self-realization, and self-trust are the aims of life.

Goldstein seems to me to be very clear in his application of values in therapy: "The central aim of 'therapy' — in cases in which full restitution is not possible — appears to achieve transformation of the patient's personality in such a manner as to *enable him to make the right choice;* this choice must be capable of bringing about a new orientation, an orientation which is adequate enough to his nature to make life appear to be worth living again."[51] He continues to say that psychotherapy should be kept free from values as far as the therapist's attitude toward the failures of the patient is concerned: "The therapist is not supposed to impose values upon the patient; but that does not mean that the problem of value has to be, or even can be, totally avoided." Goldstein thinks that Freud who states that "All that is outside of science is delusion, particularily religion", has his value system which is then experienced by his patients.

We have seen that the value system may act as an inspiring factor in human life, or that values may, in an opposite manner, function as a restraint on the integrative process of the individual. It may even operate as a disintegrating factor when the value system is imposed from the outside and not accepted by the individual himself, or when he has a feeling that the value system is not his own, and yet is forced to follow it. When the goals set by the value system are too high in relation to the individual's capacities, it may serve as a disintegrating factor in personality development. When the value system is too high, the individual stretches his capacities to the breaking point and he feels uneasy, strained and nervous. On the other hand, the value system may interfere with the growth process of the individual when the system is designed too low, when there is no inspiration in the value system and the individual sinks down into a laissez-faire attitude toward life. The most detrimental effect of the value system, relating to the growth process, takes place when different value systems are in conflict, and ambivalence in feelings and actions occurs. We may also state that it is detrimental when different levels in the hierarchy are combatting one another.

It seems to be evident, that it is necessary to have some kind or set of values if there is to be a basis for personality growth and integration. Integration has to take place around something—a leading motive, an ideal, a goal, an end, an aspiration. This seems to lead those of us who have something to do with people under mental stress and conflict, to make a real effort to find out how this works. Especially in our time, society must be brought to awareness of the fact that the loss of leading motives is a threat to the individual and to society itself. Education has to take this fact into consideration and prophylactic measures must be taken in order to create a better climate for leading motives in life.

CHAPTER III

The Actual Life Situation

It is a very common view that all our problems derive from our environment. Few people consider that they themselves might be the real problem. From a superficial point of view, it seems that our problems are due to factors in our environment, however, deeper insight into personality problems reveals that it is not so much the situation in which the individual lives that causes the problems, as his attitude toward it. Our problems arise in relationships which we form with our environment. However, the environment is not without responsibility in the creation of problematic situations for the individual. It is in the interaction between the individual and his environment that the problems arise. We have called this interaction between the individual and his environment, the life situation.

Each individual has his own life situation. No two persons have the same life situation, even if they are living in the same environment, because they themselves are different. The life situation then, is defined as the field that is determined by the dynamic interaction between the person himself and his environment.

The Term "Life Situation"
The empirical life situation refers to a person in his relationship to his environment. By environment we mean the area of life which is important for the individual, the things that are within his sphere of concern.

For some persons the life situation is large and for others it is smaller. This depends upon factors of physical equipment, sense-perception, motor skills, as well as intelligence and moral and spiritual standards.

The life situation of a blind person is reduced in the area of perceptional functions. The person who has lost the use of an arm or leg has his life situation reduced regarding motor skills. This does not mean, of course, that these persons do not "get as much out of life" as others who have more of their physical abilities. On the contrary, some persons with physical handicaps develop greater inner strength and attractiveness and are thereby compensated for the handicap.

Mental capacities may narrow or widen a person's life situation. The intelligent person participates in a spectrum of experiences which the less intelligent misses.

The life situation and a person's emotional life are intimately related. A person with an unstable emotional life, finds need to limit his actual life situation to a smaller space, whereas the emotionally mature person feels more free to widen his life situation. The neurotic uses mechanisms which become fixated and they limit his life situation. Phobias are externalizations of such limitations of the actual life situaton resulting from anxiety and emotional instability.

Moral standards play an important role in determining the space of the life situation. A strict moral code narrows the life situation, whereas a more liberal attitude widens it.

Religion may also extend or diminish one's life situation. A person with a liberal religious attitude tends to have a broader life situation than one who maintains a straiter-laced one. A person with a strict idea of God tends to develop a smaller life situation as well as a lower self-evaluation, while a person with a more benign concept of God has both a higher self-evaluation and a larger life situation.

The terms smaller or larger life situation must not be confused with the idea of a poorer or richer life. The life situation is more a quantitative term, describing the area covered by the individual's field of experience. A person may enjoy a rich and happy life within a rather small life situation. He may concentrate more upon his limited life situation which permits greater understanding of it and the finding of more meaning in it. In old age, for example, the tendency is that the life siutation is constricted, the action-radius is decreased. But even then there are elderly people who live a rich and interesting life. Such can be the case with the crippled or blind individual. It is not the size of the life situation that means most to the individual, rather, it is the quality of the life situation. Growth is a question of enlargement of the area of the life situation as well as a deepening of it.

The Objective And The Subjective Life Situation

No one fully knows his objective life situation, the world in which he lives. Since our senses perceive only parts of our environment and since our attention can focus only upon a small portion of the world, so it is that the subjective and empirical or phenomenological life situation of an individual is very limited compared with what he theoretically might experience of the world around him. We only partially experience the world around us. When we speak of the actual life situation, we mean the empirical situation as it is directly and subjectively experienced by the individual.

There is a need to know an individual's subjective life situation, over and above his objective one. A counselor will learn what the counselee's world means to him as he empathizes with him. To discover what an individual's subjective life situation is, one must accept his own description of it, not thinking in terms of one's own experience or judging the other's description of his life. The life situation is personal for each person and is characteristic only for him. It is subjective, being the result of the individual's abilities to observe his past life history and his responses to events in his past, and his abilities to symbolize his perceptions. The subjective life situation is only seen through the eyes of the individual himself. It is the main task of the psychotherapist and the counselor to put himself, as far as it is possible, into the subjective life situation of another person. This is not an easy job. But neither the psychotherapist nor the counselor propose to correct the life situation. They merely try to understand it. The question of whether this life situation is right or wrong does not enter in. It is simply the life situation of him whom he is helping.

The Forming Of The Life Situation

The life situation, is the result of a conditioning process, a learning process which is a continually developing process of differentiation and integration. One's empirical life situation is an outcome of one's experiences which are woven into a life pattern; it, in time, directs one's further experences and gives meaning to them. We experience the present in the light of the past.

The life situation is dynamic, it is changing as time passes. We shall never obtain a fixed life situation and life pattern. As the world as a whole is a changing world, so our own subjective world is under the influence of change.

The life situation is constantly expanding as the years pass by. New interests are developing as old ones are dropped. The younger generation's life situation is different from that of the older generation. The life situation in western culture has the possibility of becoming larger than in other cultures, and if we compare the life situation of our ancestors with our own, we can be sure that ours is much broader than theirs. The life situation's size may increase as people acquire more leisure time and communications become better.

In old age, the life situation tends to diminish due to degeneration of the sense organs and motor and mental ability.

The Semi-Integrated Area Of The Life Situation
In the first chapter of this book we studied the three different areas of the life situation. These areas were the integrated, the non-integrated and the semi-integrated areas of the life situation. The semi-integrated area of the life situation caught our main interest because it is the area where the integrating or disintegrating process went on, the one of greatest tension and conflict. It is the area that demands the therapist's and the counselor's greatest interest.

This area is the field of operation for those who professionally deal with personality problems. In this area the search takes place for the symptoms of neurosis and beginning psychoses, of repressed subconscious conflict material.

In the well-integrated individual the integrated area is sizeable. This person is operating inside the integrated life situation with relative ease and satisfaction. His aspiratons are not beyond what is reasonable for him to strive for. He is not living in an unintegrated life situation, dissatisfied with his actual status, longing for unobtainable things. The unintegrated area does not dominate the attentions of the well-integrated person. His semi-integraed area is rather small, and when the focus of interest is directed toward this area, he is still able to manage. He can control the situation by integrating the factors in the semi-integrative zone or by ignoring them and doing the best he can. He is the master of the situation; the situation does not master him.

In the life situation of the relatively disintegrated person, the semi-integrated area is large, containing numerous, problematic factors. The unintegrated field is more of concern for him than it is for the well-integrated individual. It is more important to him than that of the well-integrated person. When the less integrated person focuses upon his semi-integrated area, his feelings control him—he is not able to direct them. The situation is able to master him.

Extreme cases of personality disintegration show clearly that the integrated area of the life situaion is very small; in some cases there is practically no integrated field at all. The psychotic individual is compelled to build his own world which has little or no contact with reality. His integrated world is imaginary because he has to build his own "inner environment" in an effort to cope with the exterior world.

When a person focuses upon some problem in the semi-integrated area of his life situation, it usually appears in one of two psychological functions. One is an active attitude toward the problem and the other is a passive one. The individual may make an attempt at accepting the new situation and adapting to it. This entails a searching for understanding of the situation and an attempt at mastering the new factors coming into it. This is a positive way of facing an unpleasant and new situation, and it gives promise of widening the integrated area of the life situation, even though it takes place through conflict and struggle.

On the other hand, a person may respond with a passive attitude when he faces his semi-integrated area. He may refuse to cope with the new situation. He does not dare to accept the challenge. It makes him anxious. He may try to convince himself that this new situation is irrelevant to him; he is not interested in it; the best he can do is to quit the whole thing. When he convinces himself of the irrelevancy of the new situation, and he can return to the old situation without feeling embarrassment or contending with aggressive feelings, all will be well again, he hopes. This has taken place, however, at the cost of growth. He has not increased his integrated area and his anxiety then continues. If he, on the other hand, has tasted what is behind the barriers, which he has dropped between himself and the problem, and cannot get himself to forget what was there, accusing himself of a lack of courage in facing the problems and making an attempt at solving them, he has to repress the conflict situation. This may even have the result of diminishing his former integrated area. In any case, he must suffer the consequences of subconscious unresolved material in the semi-integrated area. It impinges upon his integrated area and narrows it down, since he must be on his guard against the memory of his defeat.

The most important aspect of the semi-integrated area of the life situation is how the individual's concept of God and his self-evaluation affect this area. If we trace some of the problems which arise in this part of the integrative process back to the individual's God-concept and self-concept, we are more able to make a diagnosis of the personality dynamics and be more helpful to the person with personality needs. Here, as elsewhere in this study, we are interested mainly in personality as it regards the religious life of the individual.

A strict idea of God limits the life situation because God is seen as a prohibitive agency. The God of law is the great Corrector of life. We have seen that the narrowing down of the life situation is an effect of the concept of God as Law. What we are concerned with here is the fact that the semi-integrated area of the life situation is broadened at the cost of the integrated area because of the strict idea of God which the person holds.

In the light of the God-of-law concept, many things and situations come into focus inside the semi-integrated area.

The voice of the stern God is heard saying, "Thou shalt" or "Thou shalt not". Even trifling matters come to cause severe tension in some people and make for problems in their social relationships. What these things and situations may be which cause conflicts, is determined by the individual's whole personality structure, his interests, his ability to perceive and think, and especially his family background.

A more lenient concept of God tends to shrink the semi-integrated area of the life situation, and the integrated area becomes larger. When problems arise and an individual's focus is upon the semi-integrated area, they are more easily handled when his concept of God is more benevolent. This is due, first of all, to the fact that he tends to be more courageous in dealing with problems, not shrinking from them. And then, because he has confidence in God and in himself, he has confidence that the problems are solvable and will be solved. The conflict does not evoke in him depressed or helpless feelings.

Negative self-feelings tend to widen the semi-integrated area of the life situation at the cost of the integrated area. A person ridden with negative self-feelings has not the necessary confidence in himself to cope with the problems of life. He shrinks back from the new opportunities which are presented to him in the form of problems. Because he is afraid of problems, they have a tendency to increase and grow.

Positive self-feelings narrow down the semi-integrated area of the life situation and leave the integrated part larger and more productive. If circumstances bring such a person's focus upon the semi-integrated zone, he remains cool and confident, facing the problems with courage.

As we have seen, the semi-integrated area of the life situation is on one hand, the problematic field of personality integration, but on the other, is the "greenhouse"—the area where growth takes place in personality development. This is the territory which the therapist, the counselor, or any other worker who deals with human problems, holds as his central concern. Here is where the one meets the other at his "point of need."

Are their any criteria for recognizing when an individual is operating inside the semi-integrated area?

We will postulate that the symptoms of the functions of the semi-integrated field are emotional instability and social maladjustment. The semi-inegrated area is the field in which the individual's emotional life is in a tenuous state of control. We may also suggest that the emotional instability is related to the individual's self-evaluation and his social maladjustment is related to a controversy between the "I" and the "environment". Let us take a closer look at these ideas.

The degree to which a person has his emotional life under control is crucial in determining the area between the integrated and the nonintegrated fields of a personality. The degree to which a person can or cannot handle his social relationships also has significance in delineating between his fields of integration. In other words, the problems of integration are twofold. There is a problem of *covert* behavior, shown by emotional stability (or instability), and *overt* behavior, shown by the ease (or difficulty) with which a person handles his social relationships.

The explicit factors in a person's life which lead to disturbance in his emotional life and social relationships are not easy to categorize because they are different for each person. No two persons have exactly the same problems. The *function* of this disturbance, however, may be the same in all people. It is not the factors that initiate the trouble which are under discussion here—that will be tackled in the next chapter. Rather, at this point let us investigate the function of disintegration itself.

Emotional Stability

What is meant by the term *emotional stability*? Emotional stability versus emotional instability has to do with the qualities of flexibility or rigidity. The ease with which an individual can handle his affairs is the essense of it. In spite of inner tensions and in spite of varying and annoying circumstances, if he is still able to approach problems with ease and poise, he demonstrates flexibility and at the same time, emotional stability. He can take the measures needed to solve a problematic situation without being upset to a degree that would interfere with decision-making and discrete actions. He has his nerves under control. But the degree of emotional stability is of course varied. P.T. Young tells us that, "Individuals differ widely in emotional stability. There are wide differences in the frequency and intensity of emotional outbreaks. One person has a high ability to resist frustration while another is upset by the slightest mishap. One smiles and laughs readily while another remains serious and sober."[1]

It will easily be seen that a person with a rigid moral code and a static form of religion—the outcome of a strict God concept— tends to be inflexible in the way he tries to meet his needs and cope with problems. He gets excited quickly even by small details, things that others would pay little or no attention to. In popular terms we would say that he is lacking in "peace of mind"; in psychological terms, his frustration-tolerance level is low.

Emotional instability is related to a lowered self-esteem. It is the converse of a high self-evaluation which tends to bring emotional problems under control. We have to keep in mind, of course, that an exaggeratedly high self-evaluation, together with an inner insecurity, may increase emotional instability. Extremes of self-evaluation, in either a negative or positive direction are unhealthy.

Emotional stability is a problem of maturity. It is evident that the little child is more unstable emotionally than the adult, provided a healthy growth process has taken place in the adult. The child may drop into tantrums, whereas a healthy mature person has "mechanisms" with which he faces such threats and maintains control. G. B. Chisholm says, "The mature person is flexible, can defer to time, persons, circumstances. He can show tolerance, he can be patient, and above all he has the qualities of adaptability and compromise."[2] That is to say, the healthy adult has an adequate degree of integration because he has been permitted to work out destructive feelings in an atmosphere of acceptance and wise control as a child, developing in him both confidence in his environment and in himself.

In the maturation process, the individual builds up defenses agains impulses and situations which might overcome him so that he can face problems with serenity. A mature man or woman has builtup these checks against a spilling over of impulses and emotions through a backlog of successfully worked through frustrating situations. He may choose one of a number of ways or combination of two or more ways to deal with a problem. He may use aggression, openly directed against other people or directed against himself; adaptation, a healthy approach if he accepts his situation or unhealthy if he does not accept and face the situation; also sublimation, rationalization, regression, devaluation, and the like.

Socal Adjustment

What is meant by *social adjustment*? Social adjustment is the ability a person has to meet and cooperate with his environment. It is in one sense, the manifestation of emotional stability or instability.

Social adjustment can be thought of both in terms of "intake" and "output". That is, social adjustment depends upon the individual's perception of his world, his adaption to it, and his action in it. The individual is a part of his own social and cultural setting and it is important that he perceive and cope with this situation within his ability to do so.

Most of the problems in life stem from misunderstanding and wrong interpretation of what is going on. The subjective world of the individual is not the objective world of the environment. Many of the problems of religious life are due to this breech between the objective situation and the subjective perception of it.

This misunderstandings often orgininate in a faulty concept of God, in the same way that many of the misinterpretations and misunderstandings of the environment which the individual confronts, are due to a faulty self-conception. There is, then a connection between social maladjustment and misintepretation of the environment and the self and the God concept.

On the other hand, the person's "output", his actual performance as well as his attitudes toward his environment, is the thing one is interested in when analyzing a person's ability or inability to adjust to his environment. The counselee may not adapt to his situation, not because he has failed to understand it, but because he cannot handle his feelings about the situation, once in it..

This type of personality problem makes for a problematic and confusing situation. An attempt on the part of a minister or social worker to analyze the causes of such a situation, may bring out his lack of training and qualifications for the job, but he may also discover inhibiting emotional complexes in the counselee's mind which frustrate the individual in his actions.

This subconscious frustrating material may be varied. Complexes of feeling and material which inhibit social adjustment are often related to a person's impaired concept of himself and to a concept of God which does not permit him to handle the situation with flexibility and creativity.

When a counselor is faced with analyzing an individual's basic personality problem, it is easier to become aware of his relative ability for social adjustment than to perceive his deeper emotional framework. Psychological investigations have been especially concerned with behavior as opposed to "state of mind", and more material is available in the field than in any other. Besides, the broken or disturbed social relationship is more easily demonstrated experimentally. And further, it is more readily felt by the individual as a problem that needs solving.

CHAPTER IV

The Ego Functions

The value system of the individual interferes with his ego functions. This is particularily seen in the individual's own valuation of himself, his personality and his abilities. We might say that the value system of the individual interferes with his own valuation of himself. This statement seems to be evident according to what we already have mentioned. It is now our task to analyze this process, distinguish the variables and their co-variance.

First of all, we have to define and analyze what we mean by the ego, and how it functions in personality development and integration, and we shall pay special attention to the ego in self-perspective, the ego as it views itself.

We are aware of the immense work we have to do in order to come to grips with this immense problem. We are especially handicapped because of the fact that psychology up to now has not arrived at a definition of personality and how it functions, a definition which we can agree upon. It is of no use for us to mention all the definitions of personality that have seen daylight, and all the "quarrels" between the different schools. We hope that when we have walked together for a long while, and science has brought us more understanding, we shall agree upon some very simple statements on this complex matter.

We may start by saying that every human being has an experience of "something" inside him which gathers the material that he perceives, arranges the material so that it becomes meaningful, and acts as a motivating factor for most of his actions. What this "something" is, we do not know at our present level of scientific insight. But, even though we do not know, we cannot stop thinking, and we are forced to work with assumptions. In psychotherapy, especially in insight-therapy, we have to operate with "constructs" and "intervening variables" even when we do not know very much about them.

What we are searching for is the agent in human life which is able to arrange the perceptions in meaningful patterns, also the self-perceptions, and the agent that in some way is acting as the co-ordinator of our motivations and doings. Our main interest, is to analyze the individual's view of himself as it correlates with his value system, in order to find out what this means for him in his actual life situation, and what can be done in psychotherapy to change his attitudes so he can cope with his responsibilities in life when in a state of disintegration, because of faulty attitudes toward values and self.

Some Philosophical and Psychological Aspects of The Ego Functions with Special Emphasis upon the Self-valuing Process.

In order to gain a broader view of our problem, we feel obliged to investigate philosophical and psychological thinking on the problem of the ego and related problems.

The problem of the ego functions is the most complex and difficult of all the questions that psychology has to face. Even so, man has always been thrilled by investigating who he himself is. The old Greek philosophers, especially Socrates, Plato, and Aristotle, were occupied by the question of the nature of man. In the old temple of Delphi there were two inscriptions. The one was "Know yourself!", the other "Nothing to excess!" The reason why philosophical thinking did not help us very much in investigating the human personality is to be found in the fact that the innermost agency in the personality was thought of as a static "substance" rather than as a dynamic function of perceptions and motivations. The philosophic problem related to the nature and "essence" of human beings has been focussed upon "the will" as an agent of self-motivation, and the long and meaningless discussions on determinism and indeterminism which lead nowhere.

Ragnar Rommetveit has rightly stated, that the ego's function is inner organization that aims at the creation of inner harmony and balance in a chaotic interplay of partly antagonistic impulses.[1] According to Rommetveit, the ego is a central perceptional and motivational agency, the clearing house that strives for harmony, both in perception and motivation, i.e., in putting the impressions and activity of the human being into a perspective, and in coordinating the intake and the output of one's activity.

The perceptual function of the ego is seen as it strives to harmonize the manifold impressions coming into the perceptional field where they are concerned with the ego's role in the particular setting in which it operates. This function the ego can perform by limiting the scope of perceptions and focussing upon the most important items and then binding together different perceptions to a pattern or a structure that can serve the interests of the individual. The perception of the ego itself is performed in the same manner. The ego perceives itself as in a mirror and creates an image of itself as the individual perceives the mutual reactions of the ego and its world.

The motivational ego functions are seen as a search for self-understanding, self-identity, self-esteem, self-affirmation, self-realization, self-regard, and self-evaluation.

In more recent developments in psychology, the emphasis has been laid upon the fact that the individual acts as a determinator of his reactions and destiny. Faith in the older behavioristic-mechanistic stimulus- response pattern and the associationist-mosaic pattern has given way to a more personalistic point of view in which personality is permitted to have a life of its own, acting as an intervening variable determining and arranging the stimuli as well as the reactions. In modern psychology terms as "holistic" and "molar" are common in describing the totality of the individual's activity. Psychology today has shown that the whole is more than the sum of its parts.

Prescott Lecky in his theory of personality, tells us, that: "Opposed to the nineteenth century's rigid determinism in scientific psychology that counted with two causal factors—environment and heredity—the recent modification of psychological and biological theory, however, views the organism itself as beginning to appear as, to some extent, its own determiner. There is a coherence in the behavior in any single organism which argues against an organized dynamic system which tends toward self-determination."[2]

Gestalt psychology and psychoanalysis, especially the American trends, have contributed to this new orientation in the psychology of personality. Existential analysis has pointed out a new direction for psychology by stressing the fact that the most important factor in mental health is meaning and self-identity. Ungersma says: "The spiritual disintegration of our day consists in the loss of an ultimate meaning of life by the people of Western civilization. And with the loss of the meaning they have lost personality and community."[3]

The Self and the Ego

The metaphysical concept of the determining agent in personality is called the "soul", as distinguished from the "body". The philosophical concept of the determining factor of personality is usually called the "self", and in psychology we operate both with the "self" and the "ego". These terms mean virtually the same with shades of difference in meaning and apperception, according to their use.

Psychologists have sought to make distinctions between the self and the ego. Gardner Murphy defines the self as the object of perception, whereas the ego is the system of activities around the self to include both self-enhancement and self-defence. Somewhat the same position is taken by Symonds: "The ego is used to refer to the phase of personality which determines adjustments to the outside world in the interest of satisfying inner needs... The ego... is an active process for developing and executing a plan of action for attaining satisfaction in response to inner drives. The self, on the other hand, refers to the ego as it is observed and reacted to by the individual. The ego as actor and observer comes earlier in the development than the self observed."[4] He sums up his opinion thusly: "*Ego* refers to the self as object—the self which perceives, thinks and acts—and which would be described an outside observer. The ego is the objective self... The *self*, on the other hand, is the subjective self as it is perceived, conceived, valued and responded to by the individual himself. The self is wholly subjective."[5]

In my opinion the term "self" is more a philosophical term that refers to the person himself in his relation to other persons, things, and to himself, the innermost "part of" personality, irrational, outside the grip of psychology, something in connection with the older term "soul". The ego is, as we have stated, an organizing perceptional and motivational system in personality, and as such it is open for psychological investigation.

Self-consciousness

How does an individual come to an awareness of himself? How is it possible for a human being to say: "I am me," and for this statement to have meaning? We think that the answer to this question is of the greatest importance for a person's identity and integrity. I cannot come to an understanding of my abilities and how these abilities compare with others and with the ideals and motives I have fixed for my life, unless I have had an experience of "awakening", an experience of a basic encounter with myself. How does this come about and what is it?

Awareness of the self has its basis, first of all, in the experience of the individual's own body. Symonds says: "The first sensations on the self come through the kinesthetic proprioceptive sensations, and it is only later that awareness of and reference to the body and the mental processes, makes self-consciousness a more vivid experience."[6] In experiencing his own body through the extero-ceptive and the proprio-ceptive sense apparatus, the child comes to distinguish between himself and "other things".

The awareness and the growth of the self is, further, a problem of the social experiences which the child has. "It is within the field of the social act that the self arises," says Kimball Young.[7] Georg H. Mead says the same thing: "The self is something which has a development. It is not initially there at birth, but arises in the process of social experience and activity, that is, develops in the given individual as at result of his relations to that process as a whole and to other individuals within that process."[8]

The awareness of the self is not only an outcome of the bodily functions and the social setting in which the child finds himself. It is even more a result of a comparative process in which the individual relates himself to what is most important to him. His idealized image of himself or his self-ideal will be one of the elements in that which is important to him. From this point of view, it is evident that the self-consciousness and self-concept develop in relation to values. In our opinion, the ego-self comes to a real awareness of itself only in relation to what it feels is of supreme value. One of our main interests in this study is to investigate the relationship between the value system of a person and his awareness and his evaluation of himself.

Self-centeredness

There is a great difference between a healthy self-consciousness and self-esteem on the one hand, and the unhealthy concentration upon thoughts and feelings of one's self on the other hand; it may lead to despair and boredom besides the danger of limiting one's life space. On the other hand, it may lead to hybris, as in the case of the pharisee in the Bible, who after having analyzed himself found basis for self-pride before the almighty God. Self-centeredness never leads to integration and health. For Luther, the great sin was actually to be "incurvatus in se", curved into himself—an unhealthy introspection. Healthy self-esteem is the opposite of what we have mentioned here.

Healthy self-esteem's contrast to unhealthy self-concentration is seen in the following criteria: First, healthy self-esteem is more or less in accordance with our real position and what people think of us when they are grading us in a fairly good temper. Self-concentration separates us from our fellow men. Secondly, a healthy person's self-esteem is fairly stable. It does not oscillate greatly from one extreme to the other. A neurotic person, on the other hand, is steadily moving up and down a scale of self-esteem. As Karen Horney describes it "All neurotic persons are markedly unstable in their self-evaluation, wavering between an inflated and deflated image of themselves."[9]

Self-centeredness is in opposition to healthy self-esteem. It is a pathological introspection, an end in itself rather than a means to a greater health. It may result in either of two forms—a complacent attitude, exemplified in the pharisee in the parable which Jesus gave us, or a self-rebuking attitude as shown in the publican. Self-evaluation is healthy when it functions as a dynamic factor giving confidence and leading to useful actions. Without this healthy confidence in oneself, a man cannot live a creative and happy life. Self-centeredness is unhealthy, as Angyal says: "Self-centeredness being wrapped up in oneself, inability to 'loosen up', to get out of oneself, is a well recognized characteristic of personality disorder."[10]

Self-esteem and Humility

Humility is a highly estimated human virtue, it is the most outstanding Chrisian virtue. Superficially there may seem to be disagreement between a positive self-evaluation and humility. If this was true, we were on the wrong track when we stated that it is necessary to have a certain amount of positive self-esteem in order to cope with life, but the higher the self-esteem the less the humility. That would be detrimental to religious life. To stress this opinion would mean that the more self-esteem, the more integration of personality but the less Christian humility. Such an attitude would be based upon a false conception of what Christian humility really is. Christian humility is not a lack of positive self-evaluation, but rather, the dynamic reaction in the person who acknowledges God as the supreme value, and recognizes himself as a creature who knows that his life and all other things in his life are from God. This humility does not make him a slave of everybody or every situation. He must not cast down his eyes before men because he has lifted his eyes to God. On the contrary, this feeling of humility toward God makes a man able to approach life in a creative way, knowing that he depends upon God for everything, yet having a positive feeling of being in God's providence, of having a task to perform in life, and trusting God and himself and life.

The opposite of pride is despair, not humility. Humility is an attitude that avoids both extremes, inflation and deflation of the ego, pride and despair. Humility, which is an outgrowth of the individual's value system (God) and his self-evaluation in relation to this value system, keeps the emotional life within healthy borders so that he does not reach the scylla of pride or the charybdis of despair.

Self-esteem is in no way in opposition to humility. It is at the basis of it. From a therapeutic point of view, self-esteem is closely tied to emotional health. Rollo May thinks that the source of anxiety is the loss of faith in oneself: "What has been lost is the capacity to experience and have faith in one's self as a worthy and unique being".[11] The aim of therapy is to give the individual confidence in himself, to "strengthen the ego".

Self-evaluation

Self-evaluation or self-esteem, the ability to objectify and rank oneself according to what one thinks he is and is able to perform, his ability and willingness to undertake responsibility and do his job, is at the core of personality organization and integration. It seems to us that what we have said about the function of the ego, the ability to structure the perceptions into patterns and give impulses to action, leads us to speak of the self-evaluation as the core and kernel of the ego-functions.

We must have a certain degree of positive self-evaluation or self-esteem, a valuation of our place in life, our abilities and the like, in order to feel harmony and be integrated, and in order to cope with the responsibilities and tasks we have in life. Percival Symonds says: "A certain degree of self-feeling is essential for normality."[12] And further: "No sooner does the self begin to take form in early childhood than values begin to accrue to it and it is not long before the self becomes the principle value around which life revolves."[13]

The most outstanding feature of the human personality is man's ability to objectify himself, making himself an object for his own thinking and feeling. This cannot be said of any sub-human creature.

When a human being suffers from an extreme lack of self-esteem, he is relatively unable to live a real human life. In order to cope with even the smallest activities in life, the individual has to have some degree of self-esteem and self-confidence. He must think that it is possible for him to cross the street in order to do it. He must think that he is able to perform his daily duties. Even in routine behavior, he cannot be completely without some kind of self-esteem, even when we know that the more our activities take the form of habit and routine, deeper thinking and feeling diminish. These habits have, however, become habits on the background of training which in its time demanded some sort of self-esteem and self-trust in order to be established. In daily life, self-esteem is woven into the fabric of personality and operates on a more or less subconscious level.

How Self-evaluation is established and promoted

Self-evaluation is, first of all, a social product. Self-evaluation is an output of the evaluation other persons in the environment express. The basis for a person's evaluation of himself has its basis in what other important people think and give evidence for in their attitude toward him. Self-evaluation is the result of attention (or lack of attention) given to a person from his immediate environment, and the ability which the individual has to identify himself with significant others. Percival Symonds states that: "Self-esteem is first of all a function of being loved or gaining the respect of others."[14] The Finnish psychologist Eino Kaila thinks that "... human behavior is strangely enough, and in all ages to an astonishing degree, a function of his social position."[15] Norman Cameron and Ann Margaret point out that "The appropriately structured attitudes and responses which the child acquires directly from speaking persons around him, always include evaluative reactions that refer to his own appearance, status and behavior... The opinions that the child first forms of himself must inevitably mirror the opinions that others in his vicinity formulate. He can no more make up his own independent evaluation at this stage than he can invent his own communicative speech. For behavior pathology, this is one of the most important facts about evaluative self-attitudes and self-responses, that their origins lie always in the opinions of other persons.[16]

On the other hand, it is evident that only insofar as a person can evaluate himself and accept himself, is he able to evaluate and accept others. Harry Stack Sullivan says: "... As one respects oneself, so one can respect others. That is one of the peculiarities of human personality that can always be depended upon. If there is a valid and real attitude toward the self, that attitude will manifest itself as valid and real toward others. It is not that as ye judge so ye shall be judged, but as you judge yourself so shall you judge others, strange but true as far as I know, and with no exceptions."[17] Erich Fromm echoes this: "The attitude toward others and toward ourselves, far from being contradictory, runs basically parallel."[18]

So far, we have seen that self-esteem is a social product. What has not been so thoroughly analyzed is the impact of an individual's value system upon his self-evaluation. This has been one of the major concerns in our research.

CHAPTER V.

Religious Experience

Definition of Religious Experience
What do we mean by the term religious experience? It could be given a very broad definition, including in it almost everything that is related to personality as a whole. Religious experience would then be an experience of the total function of personality. All kinds of experiences could then be religious. Deep political engagement could lead to experiences that would be classified as religious. Even bio-social experiences engaging the whole personality, such as a sexual experience, would be called religious in this sense.

Obviously this definition is too broad. The essence of the religious experience is diluted until it fades into dim pastels. But specifically, *religious experience is a total reaction toward what man thinks is of supreme value to him.*

At least four components must be present in a religious experience.

1) The religious experience touches *the totality of personality*. It is related to man-as-a-whole. Coe says that religion cannot be reduced to any single aspect of mental capacity or activity, but that "the entire mind is involved".[1] Williams James says that "the word 'religion' cannot stand for any single principle or essence, but is rather a collective name."[2]

2) The second component in the establishment of a genuine religious experience must be that the individual's supreme value enters into the experience. Something or somebody, outside the person himself, perceived as divine, elevated above the person himself, becomes real to him. William James has said, "Were one asked to characterize the life of religion in the broadest and the most general terms possible, one might say that it consists of the belief that there is an unseen order, and that our supreme good lies in harmoniously adjusting ourselves thereto."[3]

"Religion is the total response of man's nature of what he apprehends of that power recognized as supreme," Warren Nelson Nevius said, "and upon which he is convinced his highest well-being depends."[4] Coe echoes this when he says that, "Religion is the total reaction of the mind to what it conceives as superior powers upon which its good depends."[5]

75

A religious experience is thus an experience of encounter with a higher and greater power than oneself, a power who comes to meet ones total personality. This power outside and above oneself is often called the supreme value. We call it God. What makes the experience Christian as distinguished from other kinds of religious experience is that a person has the experience in Jesus Christ.

3) A third characteristic of religious experience is that it must have a direct and *existential quality*. William James distinguishes between what he calls "knowledge by acquaintance" and "knowledge by description." "The distinction is an important one," he states, " 'Acquaintance with' denotes the knowledge we acquire through direct experience, through sensation and perception. 'Knowledge about' is the knowledge we arrive at through description or through inference."[6] Genuine religious experience belongs to the "acquaintance with" quality of experience.

4) A fourth characteristic of the religious experience would be the *effect observable* in the life of the belivier. A religious experience cannot be kept in watertight compartments within a person. It influences every area of his life. The kind of religion a person has molds his life-situation.

This is, then, our definition of a religious experience: *It is an existential encounter with a higher and greater power who exerts influence as the supreme value in the totality of the individual's personality and life-situation.*

In religion, the three major factors which we have investigated enter into a dynamic interaction—1) the higher power or the supreme value, God, 2) the core of personality, the self-evaluation of the individual, and 3) the life-situation.

The basic factors in the religious experience

According to our hypothesis, the main factors in religious experience are the value system of the individual (the image of God), the ego functions (his evaluation of himself), and the life situation in which he finds himself.

We cannot think of any religious experience, in a Christian sense, without an idea of God to whom man owes responsibility and from whom he seeks help. We can state with Hjalmar Sundén, that in order to have a religious experience it is necessary to have a religious frame of reference according to which the individual interprets his experiences. "In order to have religious experiences we must have acquired a religious tradition, and in certain instances, a ritual apparatus"[7] He thinks also that in order to have religious experiences the individual must experience what he calls "roles and role taking". He says that these terms signify "the total sum of cultural patterns which are connected with a certain status"[8] He defines "role taking" thusly: "The role taking may be defined in this way: It is in its most common form a process, which includes to look at or anticipate another individual's behaviour, in seeing it in context of a role which is transferred to the other one."[9]

There is, according to Sundén, no religious experience lacking a reference system and role taking, which means that certain ideas and behaviour are transferred to persons in the reference system (to God in our view), and that certain actions are presumed from the side of the individual who has this reference system.

We may question whether or not there are such objective factors always present in the religious experience. Harald and Kristian Schjelderup state that we may speak of purely subjective factors in the religious experience also, as it is seen in, what they call the narcissistic religion.[10] Maybe so, but we are only interested in the religious experience which has a value system outside the individual himself.

We have made a study of how the individual arrives at his idea of God, in Sundén's terminology his religious reference system.[11] These are our findings:

Religious ideas and matrixes of religious experiences are taken over by the individual from his environment. Sometimes these ideas and patterns are quite rigid. The main factors in establishing a person's religious frame of reference are the home, the school and the church.

The kind of religious experience which the individual has, may be assumed to be related to both the ideas of religion most prevalent in his immediate environment and to the pattern of religious experience that is commonly expected by this environment.

The studies we have made bear out this assumption. Effort was made in my study of 1952 to discover to what extent a person's religious ideas were like those of his parents.

There was found a slight positive correlation between the idea of God held by the father and that of the subject, (rt + .12) and a high positive correlation between the idea of God held by the mother and that of the subject (rt + .78). The concept of God, like all other ideas, is absorbed from the parents. The mother plays the greatest role in the establishment of symbols, including religious symbols, in the life of her children. This can be stated with relative certainty for males because 208 of the 236 who filled out the questionnaire were men. The number of females was too small to permit statistics regarding the origin of their religious ideas but we might suspect that the father influences the girls' concept of God to a higher degree than for the boys. But this is only a guess.

It was found that the subjects' idea of God was strongly influenced by their elementary school teachers' ideas of God. The correlation between the idea of God held by the teacher and that of the subject was rt + .60. There is a drop in the correlation of the influence of high school teachers to rt + .30. But it rises again in college, where the correlation between the idea of God held by the professor and the subject's own concept of God has a correlation of rt + .61. The latter correlation may have shown up this significantly due to the fact that it was theological students who were tested, and the relationship between professors and students in theological seminaries is frequently close. This, despite the reality that much difference of opinion exists between theological students and their teachers.

Strange as it may sound, there is a rather low correlation between the idea of God as put forth by the church and that held by the subject (rt + .18). The correlation goes up again when comparison is made between the idea of God as taught in church school and that as believed in by the subject. The correlation here is rt + .32.

The environment works to form the concept of God in the individual. This does not mean, however, that the individual's own mental activity in shaping his concept of God should be overlooked. Charlotte Bühler states from her own studies of the religious activity of children, that the individual's formation of religious concepts is an outstanding result of intellectual activity itself. Dr. Helga Engh, professor at the University of Oslo, even stated in a series of lectures there in 1945 that the child becomes religious without environmental influence. When the youngster arrives at a certain period in his development, she feels, he has to make an attempt at understanding utimate relationships and to find the great Helper, when in need. What *kind* of religious ideas he finally accepts depends upon the environment, but not the *fact* that they came into being. She also has the impression that girls tended to think of God as a mild and kind Father, whereas boys tended to think of God in terms of the Omnipotent and Omniscient.

Murphy traces the development of values, and religious values also, of course, through a process of "canalization" and "conditioning". By this he means that the environmental influence acts together with the individual's own intellectual capacities in forming his value-system.

There seems to be evidence for stating, through the material we have gathered in our analysis, that we have to reckon with two qualitative concepts of God: The God of Law—Deus Legis, and The God of Love—

Deus Caritatis. We can also notice a shift of interest and intensity in the God-concept through and after a religious experience. The biographical material we have gathered substantiates our hypothesis. The religious experiences of St. Augustine, of Martin Luther, and John Wesley show the same developement. The experimental and statistical material we have gathered seems to lead in the same direction, even if we think that the results are not significant to the degree we wish. So much can be stated from our statistics, that the number of those who thought they could not say anything about God and felt neutral to the question sunk from 20% to 10%. We have to keep in mind that the persons cooperating in the experiment were theological students for whom God ought to be real. The mild God-concept (Deus Caritatis) increased through the religious experience from 57% to 82%, and the strict God-concept decreased from 23% to 8%. Even if we do not pay too much attention to the results of our investigation, as I am not pleased with it, we may see a direction which substantiates our hypothesis.

The second factor we have to discuss in the integrative process in relation to religious experience is the person's *perception of himself,* and especially his *self-evaluation,* what he thinks that he is good for and can accomplish.

The biographical material which we have studied makes it quite clear that immediately before any religious experience the self-evaluation of the individual drops down to near zero, and it stays there in the beginning of the experience in order to give way to a rise in self-evaluation during the latter part of the experience, and it seems to stabilize on a higher level as life passes on in a new dimension.

Our experiment shows a tendency in the same direction. Before the religious experience 70% of the persons asked gave evidence for a positive self-evaluation, and 23% stated a negative self-evaluation, 7% could not say anything about what they felt concerning themselves. After the religious experience the numbers for the positive attitude to oneself had increased to 83%, and the negative attitude had decreased to 9%, the neutral answers covered here 8%. We can see the tendency even when the statistics are not significant.

We have seen that the ego-concept is of the greatest importance in the integrative process of personality, and we have also seen that there is a correlation between the strict idea of God and a lowered self-estimation on one hand, and on the other, between a mild idea of God and positive self-evaluation. Our statistics show that the strict and mild idea of God and the negative and positive self-evalution is in our material rt. $+.20$, and after the religious experience the correlation is rt $+.18$, and the correlation is increased in the Christian life after the experience to rt. +.30. The tendency might seem evident even though we think it is necessary to make further studies with keener instruments than those which were at my disposal in 1952.

The third factor in personality integration related to religious experience is the *life situation*. Our hypothesis is that the strict idea of God and subsequent lowered self-evaluation tend to diminish the life situation, and the mild idea of God and the increased self-evaluation tend to widen the life situation.

We do not have sufficient material to verify the hypothesis in a significant way, first of all, because our questionaire did not ask for the relation of these factors before the religious experience. New investigations are important to attain verified data related to the life situation before and after the religious experience. I would think that we might make some interesting findings with such research.

We have, however, some data that refer to how the persons taking part in our experiment felt about their life situation after the religious experience. We asked whether the religious experience made it more difficult or more easy to associate with other people. 70% answered positively on this question and 6% negatively and 24% had no idea of how it had worked. On the question of whether the religious experience had given a more optimistic or a pessimistic view of life, we got postive answers from 66%, only 4% meant their view of life had turned more in a pessimistic direction, and 30% answered that it had influenced them in both directions. On the question of whether life was running more smoothly or had conflicts increased after the religious experience, 50% answered in a positive way and 6% negatively and 30% thought that life had become a compound of harmony and conflict. We asked about the relationship to co-workers, bosses and employees. 80% answered that the relationship was good and only 1% stated that it had become worse, 19% did not think that the relationship could be described in positive or negative terms. We asked what they felt about their life situation; 75% felt happy about it and 4% felt bad about it, 21% thought the life situation was sometimes happy and sometimes bad. On the question about how their feelings were concerning their vocation, 84% were satisfied with their job, but 3% felt dissatisfied with it, and 13% were undecided. One question was related to the individual's feeling of being accepted or not by others. 60% answered positively and 9% negatively, 31% were undecided.

The correlation between self-evaluation and association with others was rt +.25, between self-evaluation and feeling of life running smoothly was rt +.05, between self-evaluation and relationship to co-workers etc., was rt +.10, between self-evaluation and vocation was rt +.08, and between self-evaluation and acceptance by others, rt +.25.

Religious Crisis Experience (Conversion)

William James speaks of two kinds of religious experiences, that of the once-born and that of the twice-born. Characteristics of the once-born are health, equilibrium, poise, peace, and integration. Characteristic of the twice-born is sickness, imbalance, and disintegration. "The healthy minded," he says, ... need to be born only once ... The sick souls ... must be twice-born."[12]

Perhaps James is too categorical when he rates the once-born as healthy and the twice-born as unhealthy. Both once-born and twice-born may attain health, though, admittedly, the twice-born has more problems and conflicts. It is better to speak of crisis-experiences and growth-experiences in religious life, looking closely at what is meant by both.

The most outstanding features of the subject of the religious crisis-experience is a negative self-evaluation, a lowered frustration-tolerance level resulting from the concept of God as the Lawgiver and Governor of life, the great Demander.

On the other hand, traits of the religious growth-experience are a positive self-evaluation and a higher frustration-tolerance level resultant from the subject's more dynamic idea of God as love.

It is not our task here to make a comparison or evaluation of the crisis experience in religious life versus the "growth experience." Religious life has its ups and downs. A clear-cut thing can never be made of religious life, saying that it is either of the crisis-type or the growth-type. A person's life usually has some of both. One man may have a religious life dominated by crisis experience while another may enjoy a "smoother" religious life characterized mainly by growth. However, growth frequently leads to crisis, which again leads to growth on a higher level.

The crisis in religious life takes place when the differentiaton and integrative processes come to a climax. Through the crisis-experience, life for an individual may obtain a greater fullness—be integrated on a higher level. Or it may, when it fails, lead back to a lower level of integration. The very integration of the personality may be at stake in severe cases.

It is impossible to avoid crises in religious life. To state that one can live without any kind of crisis would not be speaking the truth. Crises can be instrumental in promoting health when they are confronted and solved in the right way.

Crises in religious life may stem from two sources. A feeling of failure in living up to ideals can create conflict sufficient to bring on a religious crisis. The other source of crisis is the maturation process. As one faces conflicting values, as he seeks to discern what things he must believe in and give himself to, conflicts are bound to arise which are only resolved through pain and testing.

As was pointed out previously, a strict idea of God corresponds with a negative self-evaluation, a lowered frustration-tolerance level and a limiting of the life-situation in the crisis experience in religion.

Our studies show clearly that in the conversion crisis the concept of God is that of sterness and strictness and self-evaluation drops practically to zero. We have not investigated the crisis-experience in other settings in religious life but it seems not too far-fetched to believe that what we have found about the God-concept and the negative self-evaluation applies to the whole area of conflict and crisis in religious experience.

The "God-constructs" in the religious experience of John Wesley

A Swedish scholar in psychology of religion, Thorvald Källstad, recently has taken up the problem which we have been dealing with concerning John Wesley (John Wesley and the Bible. A Psychological Study, Uppsala 1974, pp 232 ff.) He applies Hjalmar Sundén's role theory, George A. Kelly's psychology of personal constructs and Leon Festinger's theory of cognitive dissonance.

He starts with Kelly's constructs and emphasizes that "an idea of God serves as such a construct, concept or pattern, a way of construing or interpreting Wesley's world. What characterizes Wesley's situation at this particular time is that he has to choose between two constructs or patterns concerning his idea of God. With the help of the construct 'the wrath of God' and the construct 'loving God' the direction of his conduct is laid out".[13]

Källstad thinks that both constructs are operating in Wesley's mind on 24 May 1738. The biblical constructs that he has to choose between cause respectively certain anticipations. One of the constructs implies a demand for acts of atonement. The other construct, "loving God", gives rise to anticipations of faith, trust, and forgiveness. It seems that Wesley feels that the angry God demands acts of atonement that he is incapable of carrying out. At this very moment "he hears the loving God's voice, which saves the sinner who believes from death and brings him to life".[14]

Turning to Sundén's role-theory he says that for Wesley it was possible to be "prepared to anticipate coming events, as he accepted the new construct of the loving God." Wesley now was able to adopt the role "God" as the God of grace. "In this way Wesley adopts the role 'God', fulfilling all promises, the God of love, forgiveness and redemption. This is the God he experiences during the night of 24 May".[15]

Källstad states: "From Kelly's point of view Wesley had to choose between being guided by a belief in a severe God, sitting in judgement, or in a merciful God of love, promise and forgiveness—two personal constructs, both firmly founded in the Bible, without necessarily excluding each other".[16] As it was possible for Wesley to anticipate the role of the loving God, he had the experience of being forgiven and his heart strangely warmed.

Källstad can also see this change in Wesley's life using Leon Festinger's theory of cognitive dissonance. The dissonance was created, when the Anglican and the Moravian models of faith interfered with each other. The dissonance was reduced in three respects: (1) The dissonance is reduced through the addition of a new cognitive element. While the God of law and of wrath steps back, the God of love emerges and gives him, through the action of Christ, the gift of the justifying, redeeming faith, (2) The second cognitive element is the certainty that Christ has taken away his sins in particular, and that salvation from the law of sin and death concerns him in particular. (3) The third cognitive element is found in the fact that Wesley notes the exact time of his experience. For the time being Wesley appears to be satisfied with this relative dissonance reduction. The dissonance is not completely eliminated. He does not feel a sense of consonance between faith and experience and so a post-decision process is going on.[17]

The Nature of the Religious Conflict

Conflict arises any time an individual is faced by demands upon his life which he cannot fulfill. Religious conflict is no exception. Conflict is the reciprocal interference of ideals with actual performance. Conflict arises regarding religion when the religious life, as it exists, interferes with the value-system and causes a lowering of the self-esteem of the individual This has the effect of lowering the frustration-tolerance level. When the self-evaluation is at stake, the life-situation becomes narrowed. The individual gets the feeling that God is not satisfied with him. God's face is stern.

The factors involved in the religious conflict are the God-concept, the self-concept, and the life-situation. Let us have a closer look at them.

The concept of God which the individual holds may be the source of the conflict, especially since the other two factors stem from it. It has been accepted in religious circles that when something is wrong in a believer, it is his behavior; very seldom is it perceived as having to do with his ideas and concepts. It is assumed that the individual has a sound view of religion and healthy religious concepts—the problem is his ethics. But from what does his behavior derive? Is it not his ideas and feelings? Sometimes the individual's problems arise from wrong thinking rather than wrong doing. We are reminded of Leon Festinger's "cognitive dissonance"

A couple of examples. A young man came to me greatly bothered by his eating habits. He was eating far too much, he said, and he had the feeling that God did not like his excessive eating. A brief inquiry revealed that his eating was quite proper for a healthy, growing fellow such as he. It was his God-concept which was amiss. His theology did not work for his best welfare, though nothing could be said against his ethics. He was helped by a new orientation about God and God's attitude toward him.

As another example, I remember clearly an experience of my own when I was a boy of 12. I was disobeying my mother who would send me to the grocery or would ask me to help with housework—I did not want my playmates to see me doing "girls' work." I will say that I usually did the work, but now and then I balked. At such times I suffered many guilt feelings for being disobedient. As my home was pietistically religious, I thought that God did not like me for these demeanors. In order to make up for my sins, I thought I must cut down on what I ate for breakfast, taking only bread with no butter. When my mother noticed how little I was eating I simply told her I was not hungry.

My ethics were not totally incorrect, but my concept of God was wrong. Certainly I had to deal with my behavior patterns, but what was more needful was a change in my theology.

So many conflicts in religious life are due to the idea of a strict God. This concept is not in harmony with the teachings of the New Testament or with reality. God's laws will not be abolished nor his lordship and sovereignty be compromised. The laws of God were given for the benefit of his children. They need to be obeyed like the traffic lights at intersections. Now and then it is healthy to be confronted with the demands of God upon ones life when we have opposed His will, and it is correct to feel remorse when we have sinned. But this is not all there is to God.

The judging God is what an individual has to face as he comes to a *crisis-type* conversion. However it is better to accept the reality of our sinfulness and enjoy forgiveness of sins under God who loves us than it is to continually live under condemnation of the stern God of Sinai. Calvary is better than Sinai. This applies to personality integration also.

When a person turns to a counselor for help with religious conflicts, the logical beginning point is his theology. When his concept of God is made clear, counselor and counselee can together begin to unravel the conflicts. The source of the problem may be an incorrect *self-concept*. We have seen that self-evaluation is at a low point when the religious conflict comes on, and one of the effects of the crisis is that there is a tendency for it to drop even lower. The individual feels he is worthless, totally without merit.

The ego or self is the aspect of personality which most needs help. "Most serious personality trouble is ego trouble," Murphy tells us.[18] As has been mentioned, most of our problems are not the circumstances under which we are living, which are often rationalized as the source of our problems. Rather, our problems lie in our attitude toward them. Not in the life-situation, but in the ego.

Psychoanalytical theory holds that the disposition of the ego for avoiding difficulties is due to its dangerous "position." Freud believed that one's instinctual drives conflicted with one's ethical and moral principles, causing emotional problems. In the early days of his career, he was more concerned with instinctual drives (the id) and frustration of them; they threatened the individual's mental health, he felt. Later he became more concerned with the integrity of the ego, believing that when the *ego* was threatened, the mental and emotional health was at stake. He came to emphasize the centrality of the ego in the harmony of personality.

Jung thought that conflict stemmed from the collision between a person's instinctual desires and a racial consience. But O. Hobart Mowrer believes "that neurosis is ... the product of id and ego functioning in league against the superego."[19] This is an unusual view. The psychoanalytically trained person usually sees the conflict as superogo and ego functioning together against the id. He would point to an over-developed superego as the source of the trouble. Mowrer thinks the conflict is based upon a lenient superego and an overdemanding id. Truly the "position" of the ego in personality structure makes it vulnerable to conflicts. It must balance "baser drives" on the one hand and that which the person feels is "right" on the other hand. Religious thinking has usually held that conflicts stem from the ego's combat with the id, or in religious terms, the flesh. Monastecism and asceticism as ideals of Christian conduct are examples of the view that the id is the enemy of the ego.

Standing in danger of oversimplification, it might be said that psychoanalysis thinks that the crises produced by the ego-functions stems from a dominant superego. Equally oversimplified but characteristic of much religious thinking is the theory that the ego-conflict is brought about because of the id's power.

Be that as it may, there is no denying that the ego has a tedious position in the personality dynamics of human beings, being the "middle man" between the ideals which the superego has built up and the temptations with which he is beset from the id.

In discussing the relationship between the value-system and the ego-functions, it will have been apparent that, to the degree that the value-system is demanding, the ego is subject to conflicts. This happens because the frustration-tolerance level has sunk, due to the lowering of the self-concept.

The ego is in tension when faced with the alternatives of either giving in to needs and desires or holding back in accord with the demands of the value system. In religious language this is the eternal struggle between the spirit and the flesh.

The dilemma might be faced in a way of greater promise if we think, not so much of the "position" of the ego, but in terms of its *functions*.

We have seen that when the self-esteem of a person is lowered, he goes into conflict. On the other side of the coin is the person who holds to a disproportionately high self-evaluation. The two extremes are part of the same basic problem. Conflicts based upon ego-functions produce *inferiority complexes*. The individual cannot stand the pressure of the demands because he lacks confidence in himself.

This is what occurs in the conversion crises. Previous conflicts and sub-crises lead up to the conversion one, building up the pressure toward the climactic event.

A person who comes to terms with himself has an inner peace which another does not have who is burdened with serious conflicts and unsolved personal problems. The man who is able to face his emotional conflicts and solve them is able to face external struggles and not be overwhelmed by them. The basis of the inner calm and poise is healthy self-understanding and self-esteem.

The *life-situation* is a source of conflict. The life-situation, in our terminology, is the encounter between the individual and his environment. Here is his personal battleground, here his problems have their genesis. As one meets other persons, things, and situations in his environment, problems arise. It was mentioned before that a person's success or failure in meeting these problems in the environment depends largely on his equipment for meeting them.

A person's conflicts are related to certain people, things, or situations which have had their impact on his emotional life. In counseling with him, one should help him see how his conflicts are related to them. Even if they are only symptoms, they are clues to self-understanding.

They are usually the starting points which lead to deeper insight into a person's anomalies. They are useful in analyzing the integrative and disintegrative processes in a personality. They help to delineate between the integrated and semi-integrated fields of an individual. You will recall our emphasis on this semi-integrated zone as the area in which integration or greater conflict is taking place. This is the "greenhouse" of personality development. It is of central importance to a pastoral counselor as he seeks to help a person understand himself.

Are Religious Conflicts Detrimental?
There are religious conflicts which are *due to false religious concepts*. These conflicts are not necessary, and it is a matter of information and education to get rid of them. This is mental hygiene in a religious dimension. It is parallel to medical educational work which prevents epidemics from doing widespread damage. Anxiety and dread about the gods in primitive religions are dispelled when the truth about their nonexistence is made known to and accepted by the people who believed in them. Static religion, that is, religion whch emphasizes obedience to many codes and detailed laws but with little emphasis upon the life and power of God, evokes conflict. Casuistry, the pronouncement of what is right and wrong, in the church has led to conflict situations in the believers which are not necessary. The idea of the stern Law-God provokes conflicts which are unnecessary when one comes into real knowledge of the New Testament concept of God.

On the other hand, there are conflicts in religious life which are *a sign of life* and which cannot be avoided, nor should they be avoided.

Some phases of religious experience tend to create conflicts—the crisis-experiences in conversion, crises as one orients and dedicates himself to Christian life and service. In the very life-process, especially where our deepest concerns are at stake, conflicts must arise. It is detrimental to avoid them. They threaten our old level of growth and integration, but they also give us new opportunities for growth and understanding.

Conflict-situations are challenges, and if they are approached with courage and candor, they may bring us to new values and abilities for solving problems. If we do not measure up to the challenge, it puts us back to previously obtained levels of integration—we regress. However, conflicts resolved in a healthy way bring about differentiative processes which precede better integration. These experiences are passing experiences and are not dangerous unless they become static and permanent; if an individual becomes fixated on them they become repetitive and compulsive—unhealthy. Static and rigid religion tends to be detrimental for personality integration because it makes the conflict permanent. As an example of such religion we refer to a person who allowed himself to become a victim of this kind of religion, the well-known Danish thinker Soren Kierkegaard; he never came out of his crisis-religion.

The growth process in religious life is not opposed to conflicts, rather, its embraces conflict, which can lead to enhanced integration. Disintegration at one point can lead to integration on a higher scale. The only way to move from a low point of disintegration to a higher point of integration is through meeting and coping with conflict and crisis.

Carroll Wise develops this point; "The creative solution of any conflict involves a higher synthesis of the conflicting tendenices that makes possible their expression in ways producing values. Such synthesis is possible only when the *Weltanchauung* is sufficiently strong to enable the personality to gain mastery over its parts. Conflict is an indication of a weakness in integration and a need for growth. As such, it is an opportunity as well as a hazard. Religion becomes creative when it provides men with a basis for new integrations resulting in personality development and more satisfying social relationships."[20]

Carl Rogers, in telling about the place which problems have in our life and showing how therapy can be useful in meeting conflict, says, "Satisfying living consists, not in life without problems, but in life with a unified purpose and basic self-confidence which gives satisfaction in the continual attack upon problems. It is the unified purpose, this courage to meet life and the obstacles which it presents, that is gained through psychotherapy. Consequently, the client takes from his counseling contacts, not necessarily a neat solution for each of his problems, but the ability to meet his problems in a constructive way."[21]

Murphy also points out the rightful place of problems in life. "The fact that there is conflict is evidence of wholeness of a sort, for instead of functioning at two levels and developing two completely independent spheres of activity, the individual's picture of the self forbids even a temporary mutilation of the image."[22] Conflicts are a thorn in his flesh until he meets them head on and integrates the conflicting material into his self.

Religious experience often is of the crisis type. This especially involves the ego-functions as they are related to a disintegration of personality due to the concept of God the person holds and his actual life-situation.

When the conflict is handled in a healthy way, conflict may be used by the subject for personality integration. Conflict is the basis for new integration on higher levels. In this sense it is an active agent, not a passive one, in making opportunity for further growth.

The only times that conflicts can be harmful to a person are when he cannot resolve them, or when he resolves them in an unsatisfactory fashion. Not being able to solve a problem satisfactorily gives rise to a constant tension which prevents an individual from utilizing his energy in more productive endeavors. It denies him integration and satisfaction. In his religious life he also suffers from lack of integration and satisfaction; that which should give him freedom and power holds for him enslavement and weakness.

Guilt Feelings and Redemption

Guilt feelings are the product of a strict God-concept, a lowered self-estimation, and a life-situation which is felt as not operating in accordance with the demands of God or life. When God is conceived as stern and judgmental, who can measure up to his demands? The result of this conception is feelings of insufficiency and condemnation and guilt.

Symonds speaks of the loss of self-regard and the building up of guilt feelings: "Guilt (feelings) arise from fear of loss of self-regard and also from the dread of punishment. With regard to the first, guilt arises from the fear of being at odds with oneself, that is, the parents within, and from fear of loss of self-love. This form of guilt usually goes under different names and is called variously, feeling insufficient, feeling inferior or inadequate, feeling isolated and lonely. All of these states result from the fear of what is called loss of self-esteem, self-respect, self-regard or self-love. Just as anxiety has its primary cause in fear of being left alone and deserted by one's parents, so guilt originates from a similar dread of loosing oneself, that is, the part of oneself that one respects and admires."[23]

So far Symonds is right in describing how the self-regard is at stake, and he refers to the threat of the "parents within". Parents helped mold *conscience*; it functions by producing guilt feelings when the value-system is violated.

The feeling of guilt is a reaction of conscience. When conscience operates healthily there is a reasonable relationship between the value-system of the individual and his actual performance, his life-situation. There is always a degree of discrepancy, but it is comparatively slight in the healthy person. The individual knows what his failure was, the "size" of the offense and the proportionate punishment it deserves. An active conscience is, for personality development, the same as pain is for the preserving of life in the body. We do not like pain, but it would be dangerous for life and health if we did not have it. It would be dangerous for the healthy integration of personality without the conscience.

But what about unhealthy guilt feelings—the feelings of guilt which are out of proportion to the offense, which have no immediate concrete causes, which do not give relief or release from pressure?

We may look for the causes of unhealthy guilt feelings in one or more of the three factors with which we are operating—the value-system of the individual, his self-concept, and his life-situation.

What is amiss in his God-concept? Unhealthy guilt feelings are related to a concept of a too severe God. The individual sees demands of God upon his life, and he is inclined to think of these demands as being equally important in trifling matters and in weighty matters. He is, further, not able to see the forgiveness and grace of God. He is oppressed by an idea of God which is not in accordance with the New Testament teaching of God. He has, in a sense, made God in his own image. His oversensitive conscience creates disproportionate and false guilt feelings. Incorrect religious concepts form the basis for unhealthy guilt feeling.

It is easily obeserved that a lowered self-esteem is at the basis of disproportionate guilt feelings. The guilt-ridden individual has the feeling that he is so terrible that he can do nothing but wrong things. He is not able to do anything right. He feels that there is no escape from failure. And since he does do many things inadequately, he continues to impair his self-image. It works as a vicious circle. He compulsively does things which reinforce his image of himself as a ne'er-do-well. A new confidence in himself would keep him from making some of the errors he makes. It would keep him from thinking about his failures which drive him to the point that he is unable to do anything well. Self-confidence is the counterpart of the disproportionate guilt feelings.

If it is possible to localize the actual wrongdoings of the individual in his actual life-situation, and see them in their proper proportion and perspective, much is gained toward helping him out of his guilt feelings. Here is the sickness to be sought out and cured.

Real guilt feelings have these characteristica: First of all, the guilt feelings refer to actual happenings, misdoings, offenses, sin in the life of the individual. He can, within certain limits, distinguish what he has done wrong, and when he did it. Doubt about the genuineness of the guilt feelings arises when the misdoings are swept in a mist, unclear and undefinable. As long as an individual observes his misdoings definitely, he will develope healthy guilt feelings. But, if the apprehension of his offenses are out of focus and unclear, they may become neurotic.

Secondly, the real guilt feelings demonstrate a reasonable relationship between the misdoings and the emotional reactions. The neurotic guilt feelings indicate a discrepancy between the misdoings and the emotional reactions. The discrepancy may take one of two directions: Either the guilt feelings are too slight, too shallow, too weak, or they show unreasonable depth and strength. In the first instance, conscience does not react in an adequate way as to the seriousness of the offenses. Some criminals act in this way. This demonstrates a kind of moral imbecility or moral blindness. There is no or a very slight reaction to the most serious of criminal actions. The individual is not emotionally upset by what he has committed. We do not usually classify these reactions as neurotic, maybe we should rubricate them as psychopathological. In any case, the guilt feelings, or lack of such in a situation where normally the heaviest conscience troubles would arise, are abnormal.

We think, however, of neurotic guilt feelings when a clear disproportion is apparent between the misdoings and the emotional reactions, in the sense that the emotional disturbance is rather high in relation to the actual offense. There should be little or no reason for that kind of emotional upset.

It is, of course, impossible to make a standard with which we could measure the severity of the misdoings and the intensity of the accompanying guilt feelings; marking what is normal and abnormal. There is an objective measuring stick for misdoings. We think of the laws of the Old and the New Testament. We may find the measuring stick in civil laws and in the common sense of people as it is established in customs, habits, or conventions. The degree of punishment is also advanced, and there ought to be a reasonable relation between the misdemeanour and the punishment. We have no measuring stick with which we can measure emotional reactions to crime. The lie-detector is not dependable.

The emotional reaction, to failure is very subjective. What is a great sin to one is a trifle to another. But even so, within wide limits, there are what we would call normal and abnormal reactions to failure. When this line between normal and abnormal emotional reactions is passed, we speak of neurotic guilt feelings. The line is not easy to draw, but we have to draw it somewhere.

Seen in relationship to the God-concept and the self-concept, we might state that neurotic guilt feelings are often due to a distorted concept of God, in which the harshness of God and his too strict demands upon life become intolerable, and a distorted concept of the self, usually due to traumatic experiences.

Now a word about the actual handling of the guilt feelings in psychotherapy and pastoral counseling. The release from guilt feelings is not found in a reduction of the functions of conscience (or superego), although this may be a part of it. It lies more in the act of solving conflict. Conflict is not solved only through the handling of the actual failure, even though this be useful for the individual. The handling of the guilt-problem in the actual life-situation will be resolved when a man faces his real failures and settles his feelings about them. The real, long-range help, however, is given only when the deeper personality dynamics are sounded out and corrected. That means that the person with too many guilt feelings must be helped regarding the dynamic concept of God and regarding his impaired self-image, if a real cure is to be effected. Bonthius gives expression to our thinking here by pointing out that, "The creative solution of inner conflict is predicated upon the readiness of the self continually to adjust and organize its own urges feelings, and ideas in terms of the total personality and in movement toward accepted goals or values which promote the satisfaction and growth of the whole man."[24]

This is what healthy religion does. It helps a man to face the conflict situation and proffers means for solving the conflict. The means is a renovation of his relationship with God and forgiveness for his rebellion, reconciliation and remission of sins.

The idea that God through grace forgives men their sins even though they do not merit it, deals with the most profound conflict-creating situations in life and solves them. Grace and atonement both take into consideration the actual fault of the human being and the deeper causes of the conflict.

Neurotic religion, healthy and unhealthy religion

Neurotic religion is static religion. Religion becomes neurotic when the crisis in religious life has become permanent. It is a popular idea that this is "real" religion.

Do genuine religious experiences and concepts lead to emotional disturbances and social maladjustment? Do they become blocks to the growth of personality? Do they greatly reduce the life-space? Religion has been accused of these offenses. Some of the critics purport to verify their theory, making reference to what occurs at the revival-meeting with its mass suggestion and high emotional pitch. They also cite cases of mental patients who often have symptomatic ideation which uses religious symbols.

Such statements are frequently made after superficial thought and judgment and the verifying material shows that symptoms have been taken for causes.

However, there is a measure of truth in the idea that some kinds of religious belief may encourage neurosis and even psychosis. Anton T. Boisen thinks that religion plays a part in the psychotic's striving for meaning in his crippled and distorted mental world. In psychosis, he says, the patient struggles with his queer ideas in an effort to make some sense of them.

The conversion crisis experience may, as we have seen, have neurotic tendencies. The demands of life are felt as too severe to face. The ego is not able to cope with the situation in an orderly manner since the self-esteem has dropped below zero. The life-situation has been narrowed. To participate in life in the way that one has been participating, becomes too dangerous. Emotional stability is tenuous. It is not as easy to mingle with people; sociability is restricted. The frustration-tolerance level drops. Crises as a whole in the life of a Christian will carry some of these tendencies, just as all kinds of crisis-experiences do, religious or not.

What makes religious crisis experiences have these neurotics trends is touched upon in our hypotheses on the influence of the concept of God upon the self-concept and the whole life-situation. Especially important is the emphasis upon the functions of the conscience in order to see the connection between the religious crisis-experience and neurosis. Mowrer has an interesting idea about the origin of neurosis with which we concur. He says, "The answer may be surprisingly simple, but none the less true because of its simplicity. Neurotic suffering seems not to come from the intensity of unsatisfied sexual or aggressive needs. The driving force of neurosis is an aggrieved conscience which, in the final analysis, means a fear of community disapproval or reprisal. Our biological impulses are never intense enough to kill us, but an outraged community may! It is not surprising, therefore, if the internalized voice of community, i.e., conscience, has a force proportionate to the external dangers which it reflects."[25]

H.L. Hollingworth is of the same opinion regarding conscience. "Much of man's trouble is rooted in the troubled conscience. It is as important for the mental hygienist to understand the workings of the conscience as it is for the garage mechanic to understand the mechanism of the carburator."[26]

Let us examine summarily the nature of neurosis. The discrepancy between the demands of life which the conscience accepts as legitimate, and what he is able to carry out in obedience to them, is too hard to bear for the individual in his actual life situation. The result of this discrepancy manifests itself in neurotic symptoms as emotional instability or inability to cope with the tasks of life in a satisfying way. The newer view of the significance of a healthy conscience taken by existential analysis and other modern schools of psychological and psychotherapeutic thought, the idea that conscience is a necessary component in the integrative process, should be an aid to ministers working with men in these fields and to the counselees who must face both in their contacts with professional helpers. It is well worth it, to study the functions of conscience.

If the effects of the religious concepts, and the conscience of an individual, are not taken into consideration, the deeper emotional problems of life will not be faced squarely. "Neurotics are persons who are ethically stunted", Mowrer says. "They are personally immature, and yet within them are forces driving them toward maturity. It is precisely the conflict between the forces and the conscious wishes and tendencies of the individual that constitute the neurosis. In the language of psychoanalysis, this newer point of view says that anxiety, guilt, depression, feelings of inferiority, and the other forces of neurosis stem not from an id-ego conflict, but from an ego-superego conflict. The trouble, in other words, is between the individual's conscious self and the values implanted in him by his social training, rather than between the conscious self or ego and the biologically given impulses of lust or hostility."[27]

We are saying that neurosis and some forms of religious experience have some characteristics in common. It is useful to pick them out in order to help us help the person who suffers with neurotic symptoms. The characterization of neurosis and religion are to be seen in the religious crisis experiences. Religion is not culpable for the similarity. The fault is in the attitude of the individual toward his religion, or his neglect of the voice of conscience, or his misuse of religious symbols, or his unwillingness to face his situation in order to solve it in a healthy way.

Let it also be emphasized that healthy religion is the greatest factor in the restoration of emotional stability when conscience's action has lead to crisis. Christian theology has the remedy: reconciliation with God and with oneself, the forgiveness of sin, and the power to restore.

It is only as the religious crisis becomes permanent that it becomes neurotic. Neurotic religion is static religion. But the aim of healthy religion is not crisis—it is growth. The growth is an outcome of new insight, and the new insight comes in relationship with God, and other persons and oneself.

Religious Experience in Growth (Sanctification)

Growth is an extension of the integrated area. Growth means greater insight into one's value-system, acquaintance with God and understanding of His demands upon one's life and His guidance of life, greater insight into one's own responses, and a widening of the life-situation.

Growth is then, first of all, *extension*. The prime extension of insight is into the value-system, into the Person of God.

The acceptance of the idea of God as law tends to narrow the integrated area of personality. The acceptance of the idea of God as love tends to widen the integrated area of personality. As the insight into the real nature of God, who is love, grows, the individual experiences a widening of his horizon. This does not, of course, diminish or overlook the idea that God is righteous. It states only that the basic "quality" in God is love, and all his doings with his creatures are directed by his love.

Then, there is extension of insight into oneself. "By the central relationship to a supernatural reality, the mind experiences an intrinsic extension, whose first peculiarity is that the person feels by this extension of the inner life, that he has come to a point where he is able to *live in life's real depth*. The extenson is also a deepening," says Harald Hoffding, the Danish philosopher.[28] This means that a more mature relationship toward oneself has developed with the acceptance of one's own weaknesses on one side, and abilities on the other.

A special word has to be said about the acceptance or non-acceptance of religious dogmas as "personal property", what we call integration of religious concepts, and Rogers calls "symbolization of the phenomenological world in self-experience".

As long as religious concepts are felt as coming from the outside in an authoritarian way, and not from the inside as autonomous, they are detrimental to personality integration. Such concepts are non-accepted, compulsory. They are felt, in Leif Braaten's terminology, as belonging to the non-self and not to the self.[29]

As long as religious concepts are accepted (integrated or symbolized) in the value system of the individual, they are benevolent. I think that is what Rogers means by saying that the locus of evaluation must be inside the person.

Then follows a widening of the life-situation. In accordance with our theory of personality integration, this takes place through a widening of the integrated area as the semi-integrated and the non-integrated area are pared down. In reality it is a narrowing of the semi-integrated area on the one hand, and a shifting of the semi-integrated area into the area which has been non-integrated.

This process has been called the crisis-experience or the experience of conflict in the integrative process. There is no disagreement between growth and crisis. The "movement" in the dynamic life-space may take place without outstanding crisis experiences but it may accompany quite climactic experiences. There is no very apparent contrast between growth and crisis experiences.

The growth process is a process of separation from old material—old and inadequate concepts and habits. Growth is the coming into new concepts and life-patterns and the relative stabilization of these new forms.

As a person grows his life is characterized by greater freedom, flexibility, and activity. A fine example of this is found in a portion of an interview taken from Carroll A. Wise's studies.[30]

Counselee: Last night I discovered who I am and what I want to do. My strivings don't seem to conflict anymore. I see the problem in relation to my husband now—I had to help myself first before I could help him in kindness. I don't feel inadequate in situations any more. I feel I can make people like me by being nice to them.

Counselor: You are aware of the new positive feelings.

Ce: Yes and there is feeling of letting go, of being relaxed. I was holding on to old feelings, things I thought I needed. I see now the answer to many things is in being perfectly natural. I have confidence now.

Cr: You feel able to trust life.

Ce: Yes, I feel my real goal is the fulfillment of my potentialities. My place in life is where my heart is. The key to it all is love—it seems that God is so close and so real—like a silent partner or a friend who communicates with you without words.

Cr: Part of your positive feelings is one of God being real.

Ce: Yes, I seem also to be lifted from reality in one sense. I do not fear or hate it as I used to do, I just know it. It seems to have lost its claim on me. And I feel so much better. I reached a sort of semipeak before. God wasn't real then. I see now that his way will be there whether I live up to it or not. It will be there.

Cr: You know God's way is there whether you live up to it or not.

Ce: Yes. If I ever slip I will know my way back—through relaxation—through being what I was meant to be.

Cr: You feel confident of that. This is what religion has meant by faith.

Ce: Yes. It is amazing that I didn't see that before. I was brought up religiously. But I had to find it myself. It had to come through to me, rather than accepting a faith that was made for me or presented to me.

Before, I had to find escape in religion from time to time. It wasn't a real expression of all of me. I never let go. I still clung to my hurts, my fears, my life.

Cr: Now you have let go.

Ce: Yes, and I feel so many counterbalances. I let go what I thought was me, but I found the real me. The loneliness I have now is my own individuality—it is so different than what I felt before. I feel an individuality now, but also so much a part of everything.

Life seems to open up for people who come into an experience of God's love. The experiences of St. Paul, St. Augustine, Luther, and Wesley all illustrate the effect of the new relationship upon their lives. Life for them received a new dimension. Things that were outside of their concern became of interest, while the threats from within and without seemed to lose their former significance.

In counseling cases one sees that in a healthy relationship with the counselor, the feeling of God's love becomes real. The knowledge of God's love made real in a human being permits insight and freedom. Instead of feeling isolated, forsaken, alienated, the counselee comes to be released from the frustrating bonds. He is free and new. The world is open to him. He no longer stays inside his former own little world.

The data from the personality inventory shows the same tendency, even though the correlation coefficients are not large. The correlation between positive self-evaluation and association with other people is $rt + .25$. The correlation between self-evalution and and relationship with co-workers is $rt + .10$. The correlation between self-evaluation and the feelings toward the life-situation is $rt + .175$. Between self-evaluation and vocation there is practically no correlation found ($rt + .08$).

A new freedom for activity seems to be experienced through the new relationship. After Paul's experience of God as mercy and love, he was prepared for greater service. His activity before his religious crisis was characterized by rigidity. He "kicked against the pricks" of opportunity, demonstrating an inner conflict. Restless activity such as Paul's persecution of the Christians, is a sign of conflict, not of growth. After his religious experience, Paul undertook great energy-consuming tasks, but he seemed to do it with poise and power. St. Augustine experienced the same sort of change in energy utilization, as did Luther and Wesley.

This release from tension in the religion-crisis seems also to be verified by our personality inventory; the correlation between self-evaluation and emotional stability on the one hand, and negative self-evaluation and emotional instability on the other, is rt + .28. This means that as the self-esteem rises, which often is the result of a "mild" idea of God, tension tends to be dispelled, giving basis for increased emotional stability.

In actual pastoral care, the minister should be especially aware of what in the particular case is blocking further growth and what is promoting growth.

Faith and love are functions manifesting religious growth.

Growth and Faith

Faith in the religious sense is an indication of growth in personality integration. Faith as a religious term means, first of all, a sense of relationship with God. In the Christian religion it means belief that Jesus Christ is Saviour and Lord. Faith means also trust in oneself as a child of God who has a mission to perform in this life and in the life to come. It means confidence in life and in the knowledge that this is God's world. The laws governing the universe are the laws of God who loves.

The nature of faith is a "border-crossing tendency" as Bishop Eivind Berggrav has termed it. It can cross borders, climb fences, break down barriers. Faith is "the substance of things hoped for, the evidence of things not seen".[31] Pratt describes the religious person who has faith: "When one compares the deeply religious and spiritual person with the best and bravest of those who are not religious, one sees, it must be confessed, that the former possesses something which the others lack. It is not that he is any better morally than his non-religious brother, nor any more appreciative of beauty and love, nor any braver. It is, rather, that he has a confidence in the universe and an inner joy which the other does not know. He is, perhaps, no more at home in this world than the other (perhaps he is not so much at home here), but he seems more at home in the universe as a whole. He feels himself in touch, and he acts as if he were in touch, with a larger environment. He either has a more cosmic sense or his attitude toward the cosmos is one of larger hope and greater confidence. Besides this, or rather as a result of this, he has an inner source of joy and strength, which does not seem dependent on outer circumstnces, and which in fact seems greatest in times when outer sources of strength and promise fail. He is, therefore, able to shed a kind of peace around him which no argument and no mere animal spirits and no mere courage can produce."[32]

Expansion and confidence are the criteria of faith, the same criteria as are characteristic of personality integration.

Growth and Love

Love is the basic necessity of personality integration and for a healthy unfolding of one's personality and character. This is also true for life in religion, especially in the Christian religion.

Love is the touchstone of personality integration. Love is the dynamic force which permits a widening of life. Love is the dynamic force that brings into encounter a person's fully-blown self and that of his fellow-men and God. Erich Fromm says, "Love is affirmation of life, growth, joy, freedom. Love is 'passionate affirmation', something in which the whole personality takes part as a whole—intellect, emotion, and senses."[33]

"Jesus found that growth of personality comes only through the full utilization of the capacity to love," Wise points out.[34] Wise thinks that the reason why love has not been understood in Christian thinking and life is that, "the concept of love has frequently been given a sentimental interpretation, incapable of intelligent application or of serving as a strong motivating force within personality."[35] And he believes that modern psychiatry has helped us in understanding the functions of love in human personality: "Today psychotherapists are keenly aware that the capacity to give and accept love in both its sexual and non-sexual meaning is essential to the integration and growth of personality."[36]

It is impossible for a human being to be integrated without feeling wanted and nurtured, without the experience of having been loved. If this is true in order that life itself might exist, it is also true for religious life if it is to exist.

CHAPTER VI

The Process of Pastoral Counseling

The intention of our investigation is not only to analyze and theorize in the field of psychology of religion, as important and valuable as this may be. We also have in mind the practical application of our findings to pastoral counseling and psychotherapy, particularily the field of diagnostics which we feel is very superficial and weak in pastoral counseling.

In order to do a better job as counselors, we ought to have some idea of the causes of maladjustment and moral and spiritual illness. Perhaps we have not been as interested in diagnosis as we ought to have been. In order to be of help to our fellow man, we must have an idea of how to help, and in order to do this, we must have some idea of what is wrong with the individual. We need to investigate the illness of the soul.

The need for diagnosis in pastoral counseling
Our concern as pastoral counselors has been to heal the wounds of the soul, and let us admit to ourselves that this is our main concern, has always been and shall forever be. We might, however have been more efficient in our healing procedure if we had known a little bit more about the wounds we were about to heal. This is the task of diagnostics in pastoral counseling.

To apply diagnostics in soul care and pastoral counseling is principally a new way of thinking. It smacks of medicine and therapy, and for this reason is dangerous for some. We also feel that this kind of thinking focuses so much upon the individual, that we end up with a more humanistic trend in soul care, forgetting the perspective of eternity and the Christian kerygma.

Here we are facing the old problem of the use of psychology in soul care. In pastoral counseling we have taken the full consequence of using psychology in soul care. So far we are on the right track. But what we have not done as yet, is to take one step further on this way, namely to work out suitable diagnostic patterns. Perhaps those of us in this field can manage to integrate psychology and psychotherapy in a better way in pastoral counseling, and even find our own way as pastoral counselors, developing a new psychotherapeutic view in soul care that is characteristic of our special purpose.

The anxiety over reducing soul care to a humanistic psychotherapeutic approach, turning it away from its real intentions if we take the full consequence of introducing psychology in soul care, has been greatly exaggerated. Psychology in the service of the soul is only a means to an end, and it does not change the end. Diagnostics in the service of the soul is a part of a means to an end and need not change the end. Certainly we may be tempted to focus upon methods and techniques and miss the goals of our work with men. Shame on us if we do. Methods and techniques, however, ought to help us to attain our aims more directly, in a shorter time, and more effectively.

Is it necessary to introduce diagnostics in pastoral care? Some think that it is sufficient to present the Word of God. The Word contains all that is necessary for salvation. We think that all is right when our theology is right. In our theology we have the way of salvation, and there is only one way of salvation. All of us have to take that road. It is our obligation to present this pattern. If it does not suit the individual, the fault is the individual's, not theology's. He places himself outside God's plan if he does not stick to it, and he has to take the consequences of such an attitude. Looking at the Continental tradition we find this attitude very outstanding.

Man is unique. We are different. We change according to our own pattern as years pass by. Our problems are different, so also are our possibilities. We have to learn something about man as well as the Scripture and the Creeds.

Is it possible for a counselor in soul care to make diagnoses? To analyze the very often confused human mind, and to look into the irrational and hidden canals of the soul is too much for the ability of the pastoral counselor. We admit this. To fully understand another person lies far beyond the ability of any human mind. But still there is something that can be seen and understood. In any case, we may see the ripples on the surface, and have our ideas of what may be below. To see and analyze the ripples on the surface of the soul is our obligation.

It is possible for a pastoral counselor to make diagnoses with great limitations, which we humbly shall admit. But still there is an area of diagnosis which challenges us. We may say that pastoral counselors, in all ages, have made use of diagnosis, even though they did not give it that name, and we have to admit that the diagnosis was not so keen and professional as it ought to have been. The new trend is not a question of diagnosis or not. The question is whether we might find better forms of diagnosis. The opportunities for such work are many in our time. It ought to be a responsibility which is laid upon each pastoral counselor, to be more and more efficient in this work for the benefit of our profession, but especially for the good of our fellow man.

The main factors in the integrative process of the individual to be studied
As we have seen, the main factors in the integrative process are the individual's value-system, his self-concept, and his experience of his world, the phenomenological field. The counselor's task is to analyze these factors operating in the life of his client in order to get a pattern, an image, according to which he might work in helping his client to a better life.

In the wide area of problems that confront man especially in his relation to transcendent realities, to ultimate loyalties, his world-view and orientation in life is not easy to analyze. The counselor senses keenly that he is confronted with new problems in each new counselee he meets, and in the same individual in different phases of his life. The human being is very unique, no two persons are alike, and the counselor has to meet each individual where he stands, not forcing upon him his own ideas and solutions. The counselee has to find his own way. The counselor is only a helper in the individual's striving for meaning and help in his need.

Anyhow, it is necessary for the counselor to have in mind some general facts which come again and again into focus in his counseling. From these facts he will carefully construct patterns which he can use in his counseling practice. In order to render even a small help in this difficult procedure, we find it helpful to think of the problems in terms of a person's image of God in whom he believes, in terms of his self-image, and in addition to this, in terms of his image of his own phenomenological field, his life-situation. I have found it very helpful to think in line with these ideas in my own work. I have tried to initiate the counselee to answer for himself the following three questions: What do you think about God? I have used the continuum: mild-strict as the qualifications of his God. What do you think about yourself? And I have used the continuum: positive-negative self-evaluation. What do you think of your life situation? I have used the continuum: Adjusted to the life situation-maladjusted to it. Then I have analyzed the answers and made a profile of it, which gave a "working image" that would lead me on my way, helping a fellow man in the struggle of life.

I have felt that this "working image" never is static. It changes during the counseling process, and it is my responsibility to react upon the slightest change in my counselee's attitudes to these facts.

The counselor's attention should, first and foremost, be concentrated upon the counselee's feelings when he, during the counseling process, finds himself in what we have called "the semi-integrated zone", i.e. when the problems come to the fore as conflicts between the value-system, the self-image, and the phenomenological field.

The symptoms of these conflicts may be registered as uneasiness, awakening of defence mechanisms, rigidity, negative and ambivalent feelings but also a search for release.

The image of God and the actual life situation in the integrating process

To get at the factors of personality integration, the minister needs to investigate a person's concept of God, his self-evaluation, and his life situation. He must deliniate the semi-integrated area of the life situation, the territory in which the person feels uneasy and unfree, the point at which his frustration tolerance level is reached.

The individual's self-evaluation is determined by the relationship between his image of God and his actual life-situation and the way in which he can manage this tension, which in turn determines how he handles life's many problems. This complex we shall look at in the next section.

The life situation has a tendency to increase or decrease in relation to a religious person's concept of God. An overbearing and strict concept of God, whether it is conscious or sub-conscious, works to lower his self-esteem and diminish his life-situation. On the other hand, when the individual harbors a benevolent concept of God, his self-esteem is strengthened and his life-situation widened.

The image of God, which the religious person holds, is a vital part of his value-system. Looking at the problem in this way, we have a possibility to handle it in accordance with psychological laws.

The concept of God acts as a deciding factor for what the individual thinks are the demands of life according to his own apprehension of what is of value in his life. It determines the ideals which he thinks he has to realize in actual life. Life's battleground, then, is found in the conflict between the demands of life and his actual performances. How can this discord be handled? Is this conflict necessary in order to grow? Is it the task of the counselor, at any price, to lower the tension and give his counselee more harmony in life? Or shall he stimulate the tension in order to help his counselee to a fuller life? Is this tension necessary in order to grow? If it is, what then is healthy tension, and at what point does it become pathological?

This conflict between the demands of life determined by his value-system, and his actual situation, his desires, his longings, his actual performances, is the pivotal point in religious crisis and religious life. The religious person feels that he has to be loyal to his supreme values. On the other hand he wants to live his life in this world as happily as possible. This is the old battle between "flesh and spirit".

Personality integration is a growth process and as such the area of integration has to be widened. This means that solving conflict in the semi-integrated zone, diminishes this zone and widens the area of integration. A religious person then, has the difficult task of widening the integrated area of his personality while still being loyal to his highest values. The integrative process may then be a question of doing something with the value-system, in our case, gaining a new view of God, in order to cope with the life-situation and in this way lowering the tension to a tolerable level. Conversely, he might do something with the life-situation, reducing its area, in order to adjust to his concept of the supreme value.

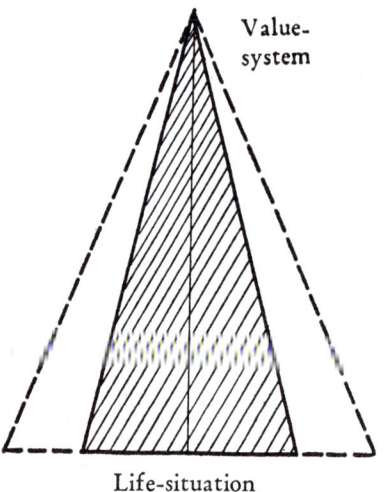 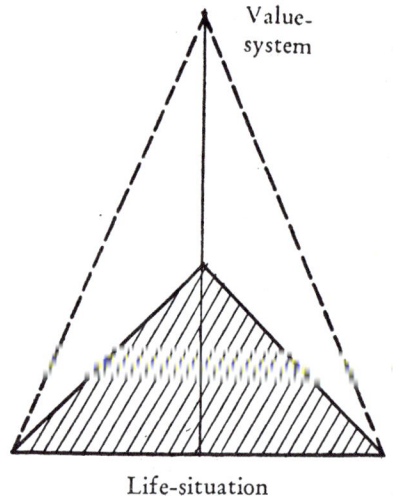

Fig. 3. Emphasis upon the value-system and narrowing of the life-situation. Integrated area shaded.

Fig. 4. Emphasis upon the life-situation and changing the value-system. Integrated area shaded.

The Christian Church has mainly taken one of two ways of solving the problem of the tensions between loyalties toward supreme values and indulgence in the demands of society and the longings of the human heart. The first solution is withdrawal. Through cloistering himself away from the world, the monk or the hermit sought to save his soul and be loyal to his supreme values. Ascetism has always had an important part in religion. Also, in Puritanism and pietistic thinking, the ideal was to renounce this world and live for the next one.

The other typical solution of the problem in the Christian Church has been to adopt the ways of the world to the neglect or even betrayal of the supreme value. This way has not been the ideal of the Christian Church, but it has been seen in the more open-to-culture, liberal form of Christianity.

The field of Christian ethics has centered its concern in the border area of the relgious person's life situation. The tendency of its recommendations has been to narrow down the life-situation to make it conform to various ideals of Christian conduct.

Soul care in Christian churches most frequently has taken the same course. In order to help solve the individual's problem in his Christian life, the focus has often been laid upon making the life situation fit the value system. Seldom is the question raised as to whether it might be necessary to make some corrections in his value system, or perhaps that his image of God needs some new trends. This is a crucial question. It is not easy to answer and it cannot be solved once and for all.

In religious nurture we have often neglected the significance of the life situation, seeking to integrate it around the supreme value at the cost of detrimental limitations of life. This is not, however, necessarily the right solution, and I doubt that it promotes a more healthy personality integration.

What we have mentioned here is not only limited to the religious field. The perfectionist, religious or not, is willing to sacrifice almost everything in life in order to maintain his high standards, which he has to stick to in order to have sufficient respect for himself.

If we now turn back to our main hypothesis, we may say that personality integration, when it is healthy, takes place inside a dynamic field, which should be as large as possible, both in the vertical dimension (the dimension of value, and in the horizontal dimension (the dimension of the life situation), see fig. 3 and 4. The field is distorted when it has shapes as in figures 3 and 4, either it has too narrow a base line because of a too high idealistic point, or it has a too short perpendicular in order to have a broader base line. Speaking geometrically, we as counselors ought to aim at the "equilaterial triangle". See fig. 5.

There is a third way of handling the conflict between the value system and the actual life situation, namely to accommodate both inside a tolerance level that on one side diminishes the tension to a tolerable degree in order to grow and integrate life on ever higher levels, and on the other hand

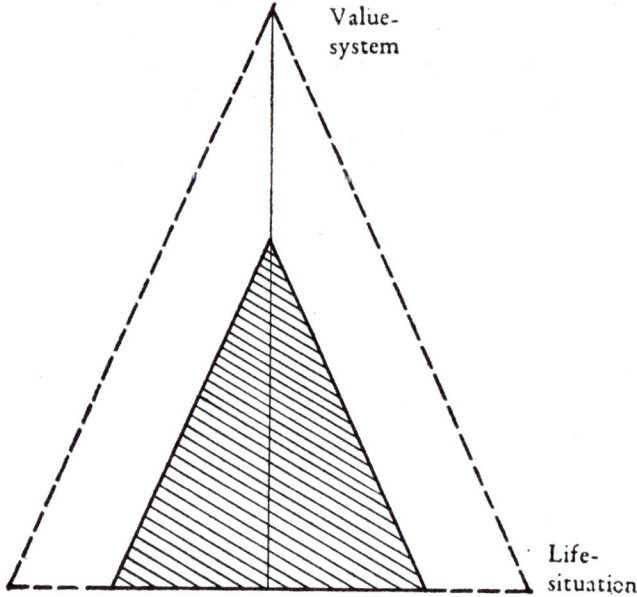

Fig. 5. *Healthy personality integration with due emphasis upon the value system and the life situation. The dimensions adapted to real actions and reasonable ideals.*

to stimulate a tension that is tolerable. An impetus to widen the integrated area must be at hand. We cannot help the counselee to quit the tension. Then we would deprive the individual of his opportunity to grow. That would be the worst service we might render our fellow man. To reduce the tension from pathological strivings to a meaningful search for realization of ideals, is our task.

If we focus upon the value system at the cost of the life situation, we end up in the perfectionists narrow path. This is a very common picture in therapy. We meet clients who are carrying a far too heavy burden because of their high aspirations, and they feel incapable in life. The therapist's task is often to "unload" the client from unnecessary burdens and to accept him as he really is. I would call this malady "the perfectionist neurosis", and therapists will in the future have very much to do with this kind of mental disturbance as the value system more and more comes into focus in therapy. This is well worthy a study.

Thinking of the religious person, we have the same picture: The individual that feels himself tyrannized by his ideals which are not fully integrated in his person. The ideals may be creeds or ethics. In my opinion, the individual's image of the God whom he serves will be at the center of his attention. I suspect that he has an idea of God as the great lawgiver (Deus Legis) who is the great inspector of his life and shows his anger every time the poor human being transgresses his very limited life space.

In a study made at Northwestern University in 1949, I found that in the experience of conversion the idea of God had the quality of the strict lawgiver, the individual's self-esteem dropped below zero, and his life situation became very difficult. When he had accepted his new view of God and himself, and even saw new sides of his God that were of a more forgiving quality, he gained a new outlook on life where his self-esteem rose again.

At times we have to diminish our life situation when life is troublesome. We might have been led to it because of the circumstances of life, in sickness, persecution, concentration camp, etc. Sometimes we restrain ourselves for the cause of what we have accepted as valuable in life, this is especially the case in religion where even life may be sacrificed for one's belief. And sometimes we restrict ourselves in order to obtain goals in life. We may sacrifice the good of the moment for the good to come.

What we have said here may be a sign of a very healthy attitude. The basis for such procedure must, first of all, be that the value system is integrated in personality. The demands of the ideals are accepted, not forced upon from the outside. When a person faces a problem realistically and decides for himself that this is the most useful approach for him under the given circumstances, he is on the right track. He can live in the reduced life situation just as happily as before. The reduction of the life space might seem a sacrifice, but it could even be disregarded as such because he feels compensated in other areas of life, and that is really to his advantage.

The individual may choose an unhealthy narrowing of his life situation which may take place when the conflict operates in the semi-integrated zone, i.e. the conflict initiates uneasiness, emotional disturbances because of unimproved material of the conflict or the feeling of being compelled to choose where the choice is difficult.

The limitation of the life-space will then have the character of misinterpretation of reality and repression. Such undigested material will operate in subconsciousness and come to the surface through the whole rank of psychodynamisms: displacement, regression, fixation, projection, rationalisations.

Karen Horney calls this process a "moving away from people". C.G. Jung would say it has to do with the introvert personality type. Perhaps Freud would term it "superego preference". Religion has been accused of stimulating this process. The religious person has to keep his ideals high and suffer sacrifices for his belief and his conviction. Sometimes this is right. It is right as far as it takes place inside the integrated field of personality. It is sick when the individual is fighting with undigested material.

On the other hand, one may lower his ideals and enjoy the "good of life", the "dolce vita". The individual may "accept life as it comes". He reduces his ideals in order to fit them into the style of life in which he wishes to live. So long as this process takes place inside the integrated part of the individual, he can manage the problem. He chooses his ideals, even if they are lowered, by his own decision and will. He changes his life style, but does not get out of balance. He is the master of his new situation. In this way he may keep his life situation intact. Sometimes, however, he does not feel well about it. He may be afflicted with qualms about being disloyal to what he thinks should be his highest loyalties. Then the individual operates inside the semi-integrated area of his life. He is not the master of the situation. He is forced to act against what he thinks is right. The problems here are familiar problems for the pastoral counselor. This process of lowering the ideals for the benefit of the whole life situation is sometimes called a change from idealism to realism, and sometimes we make the mistake of calling this growth to maturity. Psychotherapy often takes he direction of lowering ideals for the benefit of the real life situation. Religious counseling often takes the opposite direction. Maybe there is something wrong on both sides.

In psychoanalytical terminology this is called the "id preference". Encouraging "Id preference" has frequently been the main thrust of psychoanalysis, especially in orthodox Freudian psychoanalysis. Pastoral counselling has taken the opposite attitude. The superego's demands (the value system's cravings) have been stressed at the cost of the life situation.

Both of these attitudes are detrimental to personality integration when carried to their extremes. Psychotherapy and soul care must be aware of the centrality of the ego, the coordinating and integrating agency of personality. The ego must be supported and strengthened in order that integration may take place. Ego is the integrating factor in personality. "Ego preference" should mean in pastoral counseling, "to care for the soul".

The neurotic restriction of one's life situation is detrimental to personality growth. In religious life, this tendency of reducing the life situation for the benefit of ideals discloses a static concept of religion, which is related to a static self-concept. Raising the ideals so high that they are out of proportion with the real life situation and the individual's abilities, is detrimental to personality integration. The ideals become static and are felt as unassimilated elements of personality structure Too often this has happened in the service of the soul which the church has rendered. Hypocrisy is the symptom of a static religion with its severe idealism, which is not really related to the real life situation.

The aim of pastoral counseling and psychotherapy must be a full integration of personality with due emphasis upon the life situation as well as the value system, in as much as the limits of the individual's abilities and his aspirations permit. There will always be a tension in the integrative process between the value system and the actual life situation, between the level of aspiraion and actual performance.

Self-evaluation in the integrative process

The individual's self-evaluation, his self-esteem, determines and gives direction to his behavior in actual life. The self-picture stands always before him, either consciously or mainly unconsciously. When the self-picture has been integrated in personality, i.e. that the person can live with his idea of himself and he has reached self-acceptance, he is not satisfied with himself, but he can live with himself, then life is running smoothly. On the other hand, when the self-picture often comes into the focus of the individual's thinking and feeling, and brings him uneasiness and interferes with his accomplishments, then we may suspect that his self-image mostly belongs to the semi-integrated area of personality. The more one can forget oneself, because of an integrated self-image, the better one can function as a person.

Every person needs a positive estimation of himself in order to cope with life. When a person's self-esteem drops below a certain level, he is confronted with problems within himself and is incapable of meeting the demands of life.

A healthy self-evaluation is, first of all, an accepted self-image, i.e. an integrated self-image. The non-integrated self-image is always a disturbing factor in life, always insisting upon coming to the fore and being in focus, sometimes giving rise to a feeling of being quite good, and sometimes bringing the poor individual down in the abyss of self-accusation.

The next sign of the healthy self-image is that it is more or less in agreement with what the environment thinks of it. The discrepancy between a person's own idea of himself and that of his immediate environment may be too great, either because he thinks too much of himself or too little. Both might be detrimental to him. In the first case he will have problems in getting other people to accept him as the outstanding person he thinks he is. It is not always easy to convince other people of our excellence. Carl Rogers would say that here is an incongruence between the self and his phenomenological world, and that the person has failed in the symbolizational act of relating in a healthy way, what he experiences in his world to his own self-image. The extreme of incongruence between the environment's valuation and self evaluation is seen in the mental hospital in cases of paralysis generalis. I shall never forget a small, poor-looking, coloured man sitting in the corridor of a mental hospital saying again and again: "I am the Son of God, I am the Son of God!" When I spoke friendlily to him saying that he really was, but so was I, he looked at me with discontent in his eyes and said that this was not true of me. I asked friendlily again, whom he thought I was. Then it came with great conviction: "You are the son of the Devil!" I could cite many more exemples.

It is easy to see that incongruence between the self-image and what we with some certainty can expect our fellow man to think of us, shows that our self-image belongs to the semi-integrated (or unintegrated) zone of personality. The integrated self-image corresponds more to the environment's estimation of self.

On the other hand, self-estimation might drop below a tolerable limit, and we feel we are good for nothing. Here also is an incongruence between the phenomenological field and the self-image. There is always some good friend who will try to convince us that we aren't that bad.

When we feel down because of our own qualities and actions, and these "slips" are integrated into our own self image, they will not do us much harm. We agree with the statements. If it is semi- or non-integrated it might cause us great troubles.

Another quality of the integrated self-image is that it is fairly stable. Some fluctuation will always be seen in an individual's self-estimation, but the core of self-evaluation, if it is healthy, i.e. integrated, will be fairly stable.

Religion tends to stimulate negative self-esteem. This is a very widely accepted assertion The encounter beteween man and his highest value, in our case God, has eo ipso in itself the stimulation of low self-esteem on the side of man. No one thinks very highly of himself when he is confronting his God. The lowered self-feeling must be a healthy reaction, it has its basis in reality. The great danger is to persist in that feeling. Then it may become sick, and it will be a great hindrance for personality growth.

The individual has the God of Law (Deus Legis) in focus, and it is necessary for man to face this God in order to get on the right track in his religious life. He has not, however, caught a glimpse of the God of love (Deus caritatis) which is God's innermost nature.

The two pictures of God respond to negative and positive self-feelings. "When I consider thy heavens, the work of thy fingers, the moon and the stars which thou hast ordained, what is man that thou are mindful of him? And the son of man that thou visitest him?" The negative self-feeling cannot be demonstrated more clearly than when a person meets God is his creation. On the other side: "For thou hast made him a little lower than the angels, and has crowned him with glory and honour. Thou madest him to have dominion over the works of thy hands, thou hast put all things under his feet". (Ps. 8) No better statement of the high position man has in God's world has ever been given. It should stimulate man's positive self-feelings.

First when man has touched the abyss of nothingness in his view of self, can he rise to a real positive self-feeling that does not lead him astray to meaningless self-importance high up in the sky. We need to have negative self-feelings at the bottom when we are on our way to the stars.

The encounter with God

The aim of pastoral care and counseling is to confront the individual with God, to make the vertical dimension of life real, to give an opportunity for man to feel himself under the view of eternity, "sub specie aeternitatis". That does not mean that the actual life situation has lost its significance. The old distinction that psychotherapy deals with "the things on earth" and soul care deals with "the heavenly things" is not relevant any longer. Psychotherapy is not limited only to the horizontal line, to be, in our terminology, and soul care does not stop with the vertical line. They are both mixed in human life, and as such the operational field as well, for both psychotherapy and soul care. We shall in the next chapter look at the significance of dealing with the value system in psychotherapy. The difference does not lie here. The distinction is one of emphasis, for psychotherapy the horizontal line dominates, for soul care the vertical dimension is emphasized.

The aim of pastoral counseling is to give a person an opportunity to meet God and to form a right relationship to him. This is what distinguishes soul care, as a whole, from all kinds of human help rendered human beings in their mental struggle.

This encounter with God will regularly have some very outstanding characteristica. We shall have a look at the basis for such encounter, the feelings which accompany such experience, what pastoral counseling has to offer in order to provide an opportunity for this encounter, and lastly what the outcome might be.

The basis for encounter with God

We do not here take up the question of God's existence. This is a theological and metaphysical problem. We just state that people give evidence of an experience of meeting God when they confront, what they would call, the supreme value in life. As such, this experience is object for psychological investigation.

The roads that lead up to the confrontation with God through the Word of God are different for each person. It might be problems of life, the seeking for meaning in life, etc. All that happens to a human being might be a cause for his striving to meet God as far as the experience touches one or another central point in his personality, and he asks for answers or help which he cannot render himself. He has come "under the view of eternity".

There is something to the old statement of Continental soul care tradition that "soul care is preaching of the Word of God to the individual". We think this is too narrow a definition, but it still expresses the main trend in soul care, which we who stress the human side in soul care must never forget.

Our question is: *What does a person feel when he confronts God, and what is the impact of such experience upon his self-feelings and his outlook on life.* This is a question that cannot be answered. We can only speculate in terms of our hypothesis, and hope to get a glimpse of what is going on.

What is he like that God whom a human being encounters? Maybe there are some common trends in all the uniqueness of religious experience?

My investigation for my M.A. thesis in 1949 on the subject: "The Idea of God and Self-evaluation", seemed to indicate that as the idea of God became dynamic and effective to the person, the image of God as a neutral factor in life was brought to an end. In our terminology, God came out of the unintegrated zone of life and entered the semi-integrated zone. And as soon as he came into focus, he was seen as a very strict and stern God. Practically all the students who participated in the experiment experienced God as The God of Law, "Deus Legis". After the religious experience when the person feels himself accepted by God, his sins are forgiven, new trends in the image of God are discernable. His God has received more lenient qualities, he is experienced as forgiving, compassionate and loving. In our terminology, we would say that as the image of God enters into the integrated zone of personality, he has more of the characteristica of the loving Father, Deus caritatis.

Self-esteem follows the same trend, from a more positive self-feeling when the image of God has not become a dynamic factor in life, through a deep felt, negative, self-feeling during the religious experience, to a positive self-esteem when this has taken place. And it is well to notice that the self-respect and self-feeling rise some degrees higher after the religious experience as compared to before it. The partakers in the experiment felt that they had more confidence in themselves under the leadership of God, life had become more meaningful to them.

We could also see that the life-space diminished during the religious experience, but widened when integration had taken place.

Our next question is: *How can pastoral counseling profit from our thinking?*

First of all, it seems clear that here we have a means of diagnosis. In terms of our pattern, it ought to be evident that the counselor should be concerned about his counselee's image of God, as this is a main factor in the integrative process of the religious experience. The counselor will soon have a "working image" of the concept of God which the counselee holds. In my opinion, the pastoral counselor is a representative of God, or as Martin Luther has said: "To be a Christian is to be a Christ for his neighbour". The way in which the counselor behaves, his words, the timbre of his voice, the "cues" which the counselee subconsciously observes, may be factors that can change the counselee's image of God from that stern craving God to the loving Father. It is true that our Bible confronts us with qualities of God that are very strict. These qualities, however, are seen in relation to persons that turn their backs to him, not willing to have anything to do with him, or to hypocrites. God never turns his stern face toward a sinner who regrets his sins, seeking forgiveness and peace with God. It is the responsibility of the counselor to represent this loving and forgiving God.

The counselor ought to have his attention fixed upon the counselee's *self-picture*. As we have seen, the self-image corresponds with the God-image, so that when the individual has a strict idea of God, his self-picture takes on negative qualities, and when the God-image has a more lenient character the self-image tends to be positive. It might be easier for us to see this when we analyze what happens with the individual when he confronts the most outstanding problems in religious life, the same problems which concern the pastoral counselor most of all:

The experience of sin and shortcomings. How do feelings of sin and failure actualize in a person's rational and emotional life? So far we have stated that the experience of shortcomings and sin is the work of The Holy Spirit through the Word of God. We cannot analyze this act psychologically, but what we can do is to relate this experience to what usually happens in life when a person has a feeling of being a failure. Each person has standards he feels his life is subject to, and values he has developed which direct his life. The feeling he gets when he compares his performances in life to these pace-setting devices is the point at which sin and failure appear. An individual who thinks that there is a reasonable accord between his standards and his output does not develope uneasiness. He has measured up to his standards. He is relatively satisfied with his situation. He is integrated even if we must question: at what level? We may question whether he has really met the demands of life, the value system, and the area of his life situation. He may have too little impetus toward growth. A pig may be integrated around his trough, and a human being around: "Let ut eat and drink, for tomorrow we die!" It is not only a question of integration, the main question when we speak of integration is: integration around what? We may say that the greatest sinner in the world may feel quite happy about his situation, and the saint may feel very helpless and misarble. A man's satisfaction or dissatisfaction with himself stems from his standards and his ability to observe and analyze his actual life situation in the light of his standards.

St. Paul is a good example of this. At one time he felt that his life was practically perfect. This is his statement: "Not that I am without grounds myself even for confidence of that kind. If anyone thinks to base his claims on externals, I could make a stronger case for myself: circumcised on my eigth day, Israelite by race, of the tribe of Benjamin, a Hebrew born and bred, in my attitude to the law, a Pharisee, in pious zeal a persecutor of the church, in legal rectitude, faultless." (Phil 3: 4—6) This is a correct statement while he was Saul of Tarsus, his background and attainments were so impressive as to win him recommendation from whomever he might ask for it. Compared with his standards he thought his life was faultless. No one could question his high standing. Then a change of his standards took place, and the picture changed. Paul had an experience of himself as a total failure. He states that he is "the greatest of all sinners". This is, of course, not to be taken literally or objectively. This is Paul's appraisal of himself. He had come under new standards: The righteousness of Christ. He continues: "But all such assets (perfection according to standards of tradition) I have written off because of Christ. I would say more: I count everything sheer loss, because all is far outweighed by the gain of knowing Christ Jesus my Lord, for whose sake I did in fact loose everything. I count it so much garbage, for the sake of gaining Christ and finding myself incorporate in him, with no righteousness of my own, no legal rectitude, but the righteousness which comes from faith in Christ, given by God in response of faith." (Phil. 3: 7—9).

The experience of a new self-appraisal due to the change in value system did not take place without great inner emotional disturbances. The Acts of the Apostles tell about his perturbances. He was bewildered, lost his sight, did not know what to do. The familiar life-pattern was disorganized. The old world view was gone. This bound him under terrific tension.

To what extent this was a neurotic experience is not our task to analyze. What we are able to say is that the character and functions of the experience are not diminished by categorizing it as a neurotic experience. We can see that experiences taking place in the semi-integrated zone often have the characteristica of neurosis. On he other hand, we cannot see that neurotic qualities deprive the experience of its religious value.

All in all, we can here, in the case of St. Paul's conversion, note all three factors which we have mentioned as the main ones in a person's confrontation with God: He received a new view of Christ, felt himself miserable, and his whole life-situation gained new qualities.

The experience of forgiveness and reconciliation. What is the task of the pastoral counselor when a person comes to conclusions like St. Paul? In our terminology, it is a question of accepting the bewildered situation and releasing the tension by integrating the factors that created the tension i.e. transformation takes place as the struggle is led through acceptance into the integrated zone. This happens when the person is confronted with God's forgiveness and the reconciliation with him.

How does counseling fit into the integrative process as the pastor seeks ways to help his counselee widen his area of integration so that he can accept his sins and failures?

Primary is the acknowledgement of the failures and sins which the counselee feels are his responsibility. To diminish or excuse them is to avoid the reality of which they really give evidence. A person cannot comprehend forgiveness until his shortcomings have been admitted and accepted. To handle guilt feelings by reassuring the subject that he will get over his weakness, or to suggest that it is a matter of sick imagination or neurosis, or to explain that God is not like the God he has in mind, or to give him your evaluation that his failures are not as bad as he thinks-all these excuses only frustrate him, and demonstrate that he is not really understood, and only serve to temporarily patch up his self-image.

On the way to forgiveness and reconciliation, it is important to go through the pain which stems from a confrontation with the God of Law. We must never forget that this is a true picture of God, but it is not the only picture. There are other qualities in God's picture that must be seen little by little: The Loving God. It is important, also, for the penitent sinner to observe his own littleness, his nothingness. This is also a true picture. We are like that, but it is not the whole truth about us. There are other dimensions also, which will come to the fore little by little through the mercy of God.

The confession of sin follows the acknowledgement of sin. Confession depends upon the acceptance of oneself as a sinner, which is the most painful step in the process. The acknowledgement of failure is devastating to the self-esteem of the individual. The human organism seeks every means possible in order to escape from these annoying feelings. It can be done by reducing, excusing, or covering up the misdoings. There are thousands of excuses for sin, environment may take its part in it, or heredity. But these mechanisms give no real escape from feelings of inferiority or sinfulness. According to Christian theology and pastoral counseling, the only way to handle sin is to accept it as a fact and to do something about it.

What then are we to do. We can do something in order to enable our counselee to change his image of God, as we know that the feeling of guilt stems from the confrontation with God, that God which the counselee saw as his God. I do not think that a pastoral counselor does any good for a counselee by reducing the demands of the strict God whom the counselee has met. A deflated God-image is of no value for a person. Let God be God, and let his demands upon life be what the individual feels they are. What the counselor has to do is to say that you are right in your experience of your sin and nothingness and that God demands something more from you than your actions demonstrate. But, and this is the point, there are other qualities in the image of God which you have not yet seen, your sins cast shadows over the image of The Loving God. Here the Christian kerygma comes in, the good tidings, the word of salvation.

Religion is not detrimental when it confronts the individual with the strict God and the littleness of oneself. Religion is detrimental, however, when it keeps the individual in these feelings, not giving room for acceptance of God's holiness and man's sinfulness. Perhaps it is not the fault of religion, but something has gone wrong for the individual. He has not really accepted these facts. He just feels that he is tyrannized by ideas which are not his own. In our terminology, we would say that the Christian experience of conversion with the feeling of sinfulness standing before a demanding God, takes place in the semi-integrated zone of life. As such, it may lead to freedom and richer life, but it may also prevent personal growth when a person is fastened in the unsolved and unaccepted experience.

The experience of confession and absolution.

The way from sinfulness and guilt-feelings never goes through devaluation of the facts. The way goes through forgiveness and reconciliation. In our terms: The acceptance of God's forgiveness, and one's own acceptance of oneself both as a sinner and righteous, "simul justus et peccator", as Luther said.

Actually, through confession and absolution, given either through the direct impression of the Word of God, or mediated through a human being, the pastor or someone else, the individual may accept foregiveness and feel that he is reconciled with God.

We have stated again and again that confession and reconciliation is the great advantage which pastoral care has to offer to troubled minds, fully taking into consideration the sinfulness of man and God as the great demander, but also providing room for the Loving God and his righteousness.

Religion in the adjustment to the life-situation, the Christian life.

The experience of forgiveness contains feelings of one's own shortcomings, which means a heavy reduction of man's self-feeling on one side, but on the other side, he has a feeling of being accepted, just as he is, by a loving Father. This feeling raises the self-feeling, he must be worthy of something as he is loved to that degree that God will accept him as he is. This means a new experience that heightens his self-esteem. First when we have descended to the depths of being of no value in ourselves, can we rise to a healthy self-evaluation. Now we may understand, a little deeper, what Christian humility is, which on one side admits shortcomings of all kinds, but on the other, has found a basis for self-respect and self-esteem.

A healthy self-esteem is related to an experience of something or someone who is much greater than I but in his greatness loves me as I am. Here is the middle road between an unhealthy ego-inflation and ego-deflation.

You know yourself best in relation to God, and you may evaluate yourself best in this relationship.

What this means, in our terms, is that the real self-image, as far as a person is able to experience such, moves into the integrated zone of personality. He has got a reference point which is experienced as real, and thus greater congruence is found between the value system and the self-image. He knows God a little better, and he knows himself somewhat better and is satisfied with this knowledge. He is no longer tyrannized by external factors, he is moved by his own inner convictions. This must be healthy religion in the growth process of a person.

It is our task here, to see what this means for man's actual life and how the pastoral counselor can apply this on the basis of what we have brought forth in our analysis.

It would be out of order for us to say that the problems people bring to the pastoral counselor are always religious problems: Perhaps the problems have some relation to religious life, as they are seeking a pastoral counselor, but the actualization of the problem is very often quite "worldly".

The largest number of problems brought to the pastoral counselor are related to the life situation of the individual. They are problems in family life, marital problems, economic problems, parents' problems with their children, and children's problems with their parents, and problems among the children. There are vocational problems, workers' problems with their superiors, and superiors' problems with workers, salary problems, prestige problems, and so *ad infinitum*.

Can a pastoral counselor, on the basis of our thinking, do anything about all these problems? That is the question.

When a person brings his problems to the counselor, he very often blames people or elements in his environment for his predicament. He is bursting with aggravation and not at all inclined to see his own part in the problem, even when the cause of the problem may well lie in his attitude and his unwillingness to accept responsibility for himself and his actions.

As the pastor and his parishioner together are able to dig deeper into the emotional lore of the parishioner, the focus is directed less and less on the environmental causes and more and more onto the dynamics of the individual's own life. More and more, he is able to understand that the problems which arise in the encounter with his environment are not so much due to conditions in the environment, as to his inability to accept his own shortcomings and responsibility in them.

The environment in which we live may be very troublesome, for some unbearable, but the real problem is not outside oneself, but inside oneself. And in any case, we can do very little about our environment, but we can do something about our own attitude, if we really want to and have a desire to do so.

The counselor must not be blind to the actual problems of life. He has to take them seriously, just as his counselee takes them seriously, and they will always be the starting point for counseling. As long as the counselee feels that the counselor has understood his actual situation, i.e. that the counselor has shown real empathy, then the counselor will have the confidence of his counselee, and will be able to go further. If he does not have this confidence he will be of little help. This does not mean that the counselor should say: " Well, my friend, you talk about your troubles, but let us look a little more at you, you really are your biggest problem." Even worse: "You are in a bad position, but all your troubles stem from an incorrect attitude toward God. You think it is a marital problem, but in reality it is a religious problem. Let us talk about your relation to God."

What we mean, is that the counselor should enter into the problematic world as his counselee sees it, trying to look at it through his eyes and feeling it with his heart. From a real basis in the real life-situation, is it possible for the counselor to shed some light from other sources upon the counselee's problems.

Very early in the counseling process, the counselee will refer to himself, his position in life, how he values himself and his doings. Naturally, the counselor will analyze his parishioner's ideas of himself in relation to his life situation. He must have in mind that self-esteem is not static, i.e. the one and the same at all times. It is dynamic and varies according to the stress under which the individual finds himself and the resources he has at his disposal at the time. The counselor has to be aware of this fluctuation in self-feeling, and provide help in the actual situation. The counselee's self-esteem may, for example, be under the burden of depression and require some medical help in his need.

It is a great help for a person to "get right with himself", be friend with himself, accept his failures and catch a glimpse of his possibilities. The counselor's main job is to help his counselee arrive at this point as a basis for further living. The pastor's role is to help his people from enhanced or deflated self-concepts to more realistic appraisals of what they can and cannot do.

We have seen that, for the religious person, the image of God correlates with his self-esteem. No wonder then that the pastoral counselor has this in mind, well knowing that conflicts with the environment may stem from a faulty understanding of the demands which God puts upon an individual's life. We are not thinking here of the prophets who suffered all kinds of adversities for the sake of their conviction. Instead, we are thinking of all the burdens we shoulder in the belief that we may please a God who craves a larger offering than we can afford.

Here we can see how religion might be detrimental to personality integration, narrowing the life-situation and diminishing the self-esteem. As far as I can see, this is a reminiscence of the strife the person had during a deep religious experience which took place, as we have seen, in the semi-integrated zone of life. The problem has not been integrated in life.

Religious life does not save us from clashes with other people, nor does it spare us from other kinds of conflict. At time, things go harder for those who have firm religious belief. But the tragedy of life is not the conflicts and strife, but an inadequate understanding of them and an inappropriate way of handling them. To receive sorrows and pain and misunderstandings into the life pattern and accept them as meaningful for some purpose, which, for the time being, may be hidden — that is a sign of maturity. In our terms, it means that the integrated area of life has become larger at the cost of the semi-integrated area. This is integration.

In conclusion: The pastoral counselor's task is, first of all, to shed new light upon the counselee's image of God. He has the kerygma, the good tidings, God loves you as you are, and it is his obligation to represent this loving God through his words and example, and his whole life. He is the reflector of the light from above. By his side, the counselee may move into the light.

Secondly, the pastoral counselor may shed new light upon the counselee himself, first of all, by accepting him as he is, and secondly, by reflecting the eternal light from the loving God. In the light of the Loving God, man can find himself and even respect himself even when he admits that he is a sinner.

Thirdly, the pastoral counselor may cast new light upon the counselee's life situation. We are here in this world, and it is our obligation to make the most out of our situation. At times we have to narrow our life-space. This happens in times of percecution, in sickness, in times of war. True religion will give us trust and power to bear such limitatons of our life-space, even when we are forced into them. But I cannot see that true religion limits the life-space of a person, thereby preventing him from living a full life. If that happens, there is something wrong with his image of

God and his self-concept. This might be seen in the ethical standards the individual adheres to. Ethical standards and Christian tradition and what people in general think, may impede the conquering of new areas of life and their integration into personality. However, as long as your value-system is integrated and accepted into your personality, it will direct your life, and you can live fully.

And a last word about *levels of integration and healthy tension.* We remind ourselves of what we have said previously, that there must be a tension between the value system and the actual performance in life in order to grow. If this tension is too low, there is no inspiration to go further, and when the tension is too high it impedes your walk, you give in. There must be a relation between the value system and the actual performance that provides room for growth on a scale that the person can tolerate. In order to diminish the tension, we have two ways to go, either we lower the value-system in order to accommodate the actual life situation, or we diminish the life-situation in order to make room for our ideals. In both cases we have a distorted life-pattern. The counselor's task is to help his counselee find the right relationship between the value system and actual performance so that it gives impetus to growth and prevents collapse.

CHAPTER VII

The Problem of Values in Psychotherapy

In more recent times demands have been made that psychotherapy ought to be concerned with values, i.e. with life-view, ethical standards, and life-orientation, especially in crisis experiences in life.

Representatives for this new direction in psychotherapy are among others, Viktor E. Frankl in "The Doctor and the Soul", Charlotte Bühler in "Values in Psychotherapy", A.H. Maslow in "New Knowledge in Human Values, James F.T. Bugental in "Challenges of Humanistic Psychology", and Rollo May in "Existential Psychology".

The roots of this new direction in psychotherapy are to be found in Soren Kirkegaard's existentialism, and in Heidegger, Binzvanger and Martin Buber. Branches are also to be found in Otto Rank and Carl R. Rogers.

This indicates a crisis in psychotherapy and a break with a principle which is adopted as scientific. Science is namely concerned with how things are, not what they ought to be. Values are concerned with how things ought to be. Science is interested in quantities, how things may be measured and counted and generalized, not with qualities, the essence of things. This last area belongs to philosophy and religion, not science.

It is most interesting to see that in psychoanalysis, we find a very clear development in the direction of an increasing accentuation upon the problem of values. In the first period of psychoanalysis, following Freud's own description, which we label, the libido-determined period, emphasis is laid, upon the sexual (libido) components. Here the emphasis is laid upon the *intra-psychic* tension between super-ego and id. The next period in psychoanalysis is characterized by the *interpersonal* relations. This is the socio-cultural period. This tendency may be traced back to Alfred Adler. Most explicitly it is to be found in the American branch of psychoanalysis represented by Harry Stack Sullivan, Karen Horney, Erich Fromm, Alexander, French, Erik Homburger Erikson, and others. The third period is characterized by stressing values and meaning. We might call this period the noogene or *existential* period. Representatives of this trend are Viktor E. Frankl, A.H. Maslow, Hobart Mowrer, and others. We may say that, here emphasis is laid upon *super-individual* values, ultimate loyalities.

In client-centered therapy, the development is also evident. Carl R. Rogers has in more recent years concentrated more and more on value problems in psychotherapy. In an article "Toward a Modern Approach to Values" he writes: "There is a great deal of concern today with the problem of values. Youth, in almost every country, is deeply uncertain of its value orientation; the values associated with various religions have lost much of their influence; sophisticated individuals in every culture seem unsure and troubled as to the goals they hold in esteem. The reasons are not far to seek. The whole culture, in all its aspects seems increasingly scientific and relativistic, and the rigid, absolute views on values which come to us from the past appear anachronistic. Even more important, perhaps, is the fact that the modern individual is assailed from every angle by divergent and contradictory value claims. It is no longer possible, as it was in the not too distant historical past, to settle comfortably into the value system of one's forebears or one's community and live out one's life without ever examining the nature and the assumptions of that system."[1]

Rogers continues in stating that the problems of values actualize themselves particularily in psychotherapy "As with other issues the general problem faced by the culture is painfully and specifically evident in the cultural microcosm which is called the therapeutic relationship, which is my sphere of experience."[2]

He thinks that experiences in psychotherapy give him opportunity to say: "... I believe I see some directional threads emerging which might offer a new concept of the valuing process, more tenable in the modern world."[3] Then he shows how the human being is building up his own system of values by introjecting impressions from his environment, and afterwards arrives at, what he calls, "the locus of evaluation in himself", i.e. he experiences that the value system is a vital part of himself, he dares to stand up for it even against the pressure that his environment exercises upon him in opposite directions.

Rogers concludes his article by saying: "Finally, it appears that we have returned to the issue of universality of values, but by a different route. Instead of universal values "out there", or universal value system imposed by some group—philosophers, rulers, priests, or psychologists—we have the possibility of universal human value directions emerging from the experiencing of the human organism. Evidence from therapy indicates that both personal and social values emerge as natural, and experienced, when the individual is close to his own organismic valuing process. The suggestion is that though modern man no longer trusts religion or science or philosophy nor any system of beliefs to give him values, he may find an organismic valuing base within himself which, if he can learn again to be in touch with it, will prove to be an organized, adaptive, and social approach to the perplexing value issues which face all of us."[4]

We have quoted so much from this article on values by Rogers mostly to show that the value problem in psychotherapy has gained a very prominent place in his thinking. On the other hand, we cannot share his viewpoints. They are too pragmatic and individualistic, forgetting traditions which we also have when we speak of values. And one more point. Rogers forgets that traditional value systems may be integrated in personality and serve as promotors of meaningful life. We do not share Rogers' distrust of religion, science and philosophy as if they were unable to create and structure systems of value which may seem meaningful to man. We do not think that the problem of value can be solved solely on the empirical and inductive level. Some trends from human history will always mingle with our own valuing processes. And the great question is, what shall we do with these? In our opinion, they must either be integrated in personality or skipped, and this process must go on together with our own organismic valuing processes.

I doubt that if each person built-up his own system of values, as Rogers states, and we put all these individual systems of values together, that they would provide us with guidelines that would be socially acceptable. In my mind, we have to reach a synthesis between the value systems that stem from the experience which generations before us have had, exemplified in convictions and creeds, and our own valuing procedure, and integrate this complex matter into our own personality, signing it with our own names. This sounds much better to me, even if it is more difficult. We cannot easily ignore the insight into problems of values which our ancestors have arrived at. When we are dissatisfied with the older formulations of values, we may develop new ones according to our own decisions, but we cannot simply ignore them as if they never had been. To build our own value systems, simply upon empirical data from our own arsenal, seems to me to be too superficial. Our concern must also be, foremost, to consider our heritage concerning values in our strivings to get at our own value system, not only to listen to our own heart. We might then be lead astray.

*The possibility to introduce values in psychotherapy
not violating the scientific base*

First of all, we would like to ask whether it is possible, on the whole, to avoid introducing values in psychotherapy. Is it possible to have therapy with a client for a longer period of time without touching his value system and not doing anything in order to handle the problem? It is one thing if I, as a therapist, introduce values into the therapeutic process, and even worse, if I force my client to take over my own value system, and quite another to meet my client's value and react to it.

Very soon we shall realize that the therapist in his work always operates with values. He seeks certain goals in his practice, and the goals are fixed on the basis of his own values, what he thinks is good and beneficial for his client. These goals he seeks to fulfill in therapy. The therapist's motivation for what he is doing has to do with values, his own values. He has, however, also learned to listen to the client's formulation of what he thinks is of value to him, what is steering his life process, determines the levels of aspiration, sometimes as an inspiration and as an integrating part of personalty development, and sometimes as a threat and frustration in the individual as he is striving to grow. Sometimes it happens that different value systems are in conflict with one another, and this initiates disintegration.

The real problem seems to arise when we begin to establish hierarchies of values, as Maslow does. These hierarchies must, by definition, be subjective even when they might seem to stem from accepted values in the environment, traditions, and conventions.

At first we have the problem of the therapist's own search for his value system. He can not avoid this. If he is to operate as a therapist, he has to have some kind of order in his own value-hierarchy. This value-hierarchy will function in his therapeutic practice as a reference system, not only for himself, but for his client as well. A therapist without an integrated value system is handicapped in his therapeutic practice.

Then comes the problem of how the therapist should make use of his own value system in therapy. Our opinion is that he shall use his value system as a reference system, as a means of comparison which his client may use, if he wishes, as the client is working on establishing and correcting his own value system. The therapist may go so far, under special circumstances, that he lends his value system in a critical situation during the process of therapy, to the client who is not able to see or to establish his own value system. Examples of this procedure may be taken from therapy with alcoholics and narcotics. Limits have to be set for the use of the therapist's value system in the therapeutic process. In no case must this be felt by the client as a demand or as pressure. Under all circumstances the therapist must have the greatest respect for the value system of the client, be it so confused as it sometimes might be.

It seems clear that as the value hierarchy leads to its peak, what Paul Tillich calls "The supreme value", or "ultimate concern", the empirical basis is broken and the road is open for speculations in philosophy and religion. Then, according to the old receipt, psychotherapy has passed its given limits.

The problems mentioned here and many others press on for analyzis and answer. It seems to be possible to do something with it in our time. Let us do it!

So far, we have stated that we have to work with values in therapy. We have further mentioned that it is not in the interest of psychotherapy to speculate in philosophical and theological value systems. This is the job of the philosopher and the minister. It is convenient and important for psychotherapy to work with what Rogers calls "operative values", i.e. values that work in the actual situation, in the phenomenological world. This field is open to analysis and quantitative measurement.

An experiment in treating values in psychotherapy
A diagnostic design

My interest in value problematics in psychotherapy has grown out of studies in pastoral counseling and my teaching and practicing psychotherapy for many years. It seems to me that here we are operating in a field that is vital both for pastoral counseling and psychotherapy. Maybe we could profit on both sides through co-operation.

In my dissertation on "The Idea of God and Personality Integration" I made an experiment in order to analyze the impact of a person's religious ideas (values) upon his personality integration with special reference to his self-evaluation and his experience of how he functioned in life, his life-situation.[5]

In getting at the individual's value system, especially "the supreme value" which for a religious person, must be his God, I could experimentally show a change in self-evaluation. The strict idea of God correlated with a negative self-evaluation, which again correlated with a narrowing of the life-space. On the other hand, we found positive correlation between the mild idea of God and enhancement of the self-feeling and increased life-space.

For the religious person, the value system may work in an integrating way with heightening of self-feeling and widening of the life-situation. It may, however, also work in the opposite direction as a disintegrating factor lowering the self-feeling and reducing the life-space.

It struck me that these findings might be useful in broader sense and applied to psychotherapy in the cases where the value system plays an important role in establishing neuroses and mental disturbances.

Refering to the models on pages 104 and 106, we may say that the therapist may use these as a diagnostic design. The therapist may register the value-system of the client and arrive at the client's value-hierarchy, as we did in our research using a five-point scale. He might do the same with the self-evaluation of the client and his concept of his life-situation. The therapist will then get an idea of when these factors disturb the client. In our terminology, the dynamic process is going on in the semi-integrated zone. We may also think of this in terms of Murphy's value-hierarchy and anxiety-hierarchy.

The critical point on the scale is attained when the client feels himself tense as he is facing the ideals to which he feels himself submitted. Then the client reacts with anxiety.

Obtaining a profile of the client's value-system, his self-evaluation, and his life-situation, is a question of intent listening on the part of the therapist, taking notice of the slightest emotional expression by the client. We think that the therapist will get three different profiles. First, we have the *idealist* or *perfectionist* who places his goals very high, and he cannot bear the burden of lowering them. Usually he has to pay for his high aspirations, sacrificing parts of his life-space. This is the way in which he can handle the tension which he feels between his ideals and his actual life. We find examples of this attitude in the religious or political fanatic, the moral-preacher, the monk, and the ascetic. On the other hand, we have the *bohemian* who easily takes what he can get of the worldly goods, but he does not take his obligations too seriously. He can manage the tension by closing his eyes to the demands of his value system, if he has one. Thirdly, we have the *integrated* type, who has arrived at a fairly stable balance between ideals and practical life. Here we have the practical individual who has arrived at a value system that does not create unnecessary conflicts with his actual performance but still gives impetus for growth.

We may also speak of levels of integration, which may be seen, not in the shape of the triangle but in its form, if we stick to our diagrams.

The perfectionist neurosis

The perfectionist neurosis has to do with the individual's value system. The crucial point in diagnosis and in therapy is for the therapist to help his client to understand how the value system is operating in his life in relation to his actual life-situation, to see how the ideal world of the client correlates to his abilities, how his strivings are related to his doings. On the one hand, he should not lower the value system so that a situation of apathy occurs, and, on the other hand, he should not raise the demands of the value system to such a degree that stress symptoms occur and a psychological tension takes place, which tends to paralyze the functions of the client. To find this level of aspiration is the problem of personality integration. It is not easy to find, and it has to be rediscovered and regulated time and again.

The demands of the value system may be, as we have seen, too high or too low. Here we are concerned with the problem of the value system demanding too much of the individual. Thus we are facing, what we would call, the perfectionist neurosis. What has been a natural impulse, namely to perform his best, has become a threat to the client, an overwhelming demand upon his effectivity which limits his life-space and narrows his activities. He has loaded himself with burdens that are too heavy for him, and in most cases unnecessary to bear. The client finds himself caught in a vicious circle: The more he feels the demands of his value system, the more he narrows his life-space, and the more he narrows his life-space the heavier the demands of the value system become.

It seems to me that the demands of effectivity in our time are increasing this stress situation. It is not only a situation which we face in soul-care, when the cravings of God are felt as unbearable, it is an overall experience of people in our society today. There are more people suffering from the perfectionist neurosis today than we would imagine.

The therapist ought to be keenly aware of the dynamics going on in his client as he suffers from the perfectionist neurosis. We humbly admit that this is not an easy job, because the client will hide behind strong defenses, which is a part of his pattern in which the value system plays an important role, and serves the function of keeping his anxieties on a tolerable level. Further, it is evident that the client's value system is an important part of his deepest personal secrets. This means that he is not, at first, willing to bring it to the surface, and when it comes up, it is disguised because of rationalization. Perhaps he is not able to clearly see his own value system and accept it. It is operating on the subconscious level, encumbered with guilt-feelings and a need for atonement. Brought into the daylight in the therapeutic process, he cannot recognize it.

How do we get at the value system of the client? It seems to me, after dealing with actual cases of the perfectionist neurosis, that it is the first concern of the therapist to analyze the client's life-space. Here the problems are actualized. The client will easily bring things, occurrences from his daily life, into the interview. Something in his actual life-situation was the reason for his coming to therapy. The symptoms of the neurosis are to be seen in the actual life-situation.

The next step for the therapist to take, is to look for the client's self-esteem, his opinion of himself, which may be done through personality tests in addition to what the listening ear of the therapist may get out of the interview.

In my view and practice, these are the roads that lead to the analysis of the client's value system. It is usually problematic to arrive at the clients' value system immediately. Generally the client is unwilling to communicate his highest loyalties. It concerns his intermost secrets, the center of his personality. You will get at the value system of the client as he reveals parts of his history, his childhood and especially his adolescent years, what he feels about his parents and significant persons who have played an important role in his life. He will reveal his likes and dislikes as the interview goes on, his needs and longings, his feelings of loyalty to someone that means something to him. If you can get at the client's feelings as he finds himself in crisis experiences in his life, you will probably get at parts of his value system. My feeling is that the deeper the therapist goes into the emotional life of his client, the closer he comes to his value system. No person bears his value system visibly on his breast. You have to go deeper if you are in search of it, and you have to walk a long way and sometimes take detours in order to find the secrets of personality as they are related to his value system. It is, however, well worth the trouble and the patience needed.

Therapy with problems of values

We have come to the conclusion that the value system of an individual serving as a leading principle of life, is a deciding factor in his apprehension of himself and his world, his attitudes both toward himself and his fellow man. The value system is thus, a basic factor in the integration or disintegration of personality.

It is our obligation as psychotherapists to take into consideration these facts. How to analyze (make diagnosis) in the actual situation is our concern, but, most of all, we have to find ways in which we can handle the problems of integration and disintegration in personal life where the causes are to be found in basic loyalties.

This has been the concern of the pastoral counselor all the time, and he has had his answers. It is my feeling that the time has come for psychotherapists to meet and discuss these problems. Let us have a look at our findings in order to find some help in this challenging area.

The treatment of value problems in therapy is, in my opinion, the most challenging and difficult of all the problems that arise in therapy. It is difficult to get at them, and it is problematic to treat them.

The first question here is *who shall take the initiative* bringing forth the problem of values in the therapeutic process? This question is easy to answer on the basis of client-centered therapy. The initiative is in the hand of the client. It should not be necessary to say this, but thinking of our own interest in presenting our own value systems and working as pedagogues and missionaries, it is necessary to emphasize the fact. We must make a distinction between pastoral care and psychotherapy. The pastoral counselor has a greater freedom to present his value system to the client than the therapist has, even though here we will also give a word of caution.

It is in the junction where psychotherapy and pastoral counseling meet that the problem of value arises. The main areas in pastoral counseling are life-view problems and life orientation. This gives the counselor freer hands to "treat" persons with these problems. As therapists we have something to learn here, but we have also a problem which we have to solve.

If psychotherapy is interested in the whole human being, the therapist cannot avoid considering and finding an answer to the problem of values, as a great part of emotional problems have to do with the life-view problematics.

In pastoral counseling the concern is with life-view problems, especially questions like these: Where did I come from? Why am I here? Is there any meaning to life at all? What is the goal of life? Where is God? How does he act? The pastoral counselor must be free to play on the whole register.

With the therapist the position is another. He has to show a certain degree of neutrality in life-view problems. He should not provoke the problems, but, on the other hand, he should not and cannot hide himself in his psychological ivory tower and say, as did the sheriff in the play "Brand" by Ibsen: "This does not belong to my district". There is no such thing as the "neutral observer" in psychotherapy any longer. Likewise, "the active observer" no longer exists. The therapist has to be "partaker" in the therapeutic process, as we shall see later in this chapter. Without regard to the "school" to which the therapist feels he belongs, he has to participate in the fight which his client is fighting in order to shed light and insight upon the deepest problems of life. The question is how far or how deep he should dig into the problems of life and values. In my opinion, the answer is quite simple. The therapist should walk as far on this narrow road as the client permits him to. In practice this means that the client always has the initiative. If the client's problems touch the value system and their practical application to life, the therapist has to follow him on his severe voyage to insight and new orientation with the qualifications and personal equipment he has.

When the therapist feels that he has arrived at the limits of his abilities in helping a person with his life-view troubles, he has to admit this to himself and to his client and then refer the client to someone else who can do a better job. My feeling is that the pastoral counselor generally is better off here than the therapist, and why not refer to him? There is no disparagement in such procedure. We all have our special fields, one is better in one field than the other. All that a therapist can do to better deal with life-view problems is to work on his own personality and clarify his own attitudes toward life and what he values most. This is his obligation in order not to get into conflict with himself when value problems come to the fore in therapy, which will prevent him from doing a positive job. He must admit that his own value system will be revealed in the therapeutic process either consciously or unconsciously. The therapist's life-view will serve as a reference system in therapy. You can help others with their life problems only as far as you have been helped with your own problems of life.

The next point is that the therapist must be keenly aware of the fact that it is not his life-view and his own solution to his life problems that is to be demonstrated or handled. All the time the focus is upon the values of the client. The therapist should not, of course, hide his own life-view. He ought to be honest to himself also in this respect. If he is genuine and transparent, his life-view will shine through. The therapist has to act with his whole personality in therapy. How can he do this without playing out his main life attitude in the interview? The therapist must be aware of the fact that he may only use his life-view as a reference system, not as a dogmatic system which another person has to accept or is forced into.

What we have said here may be of importance for our therapy. We have stated previously that psychotherapy often heals the existential sufferings of the individual by taking special interest in the life situation, neglecting the values of the individual. We think that it would be a step in the right direction in psychoterapy, if it was more concerned with values.

As a conclusion we would like to mention the following facts: Neglecting value problematics means that therapy cannot fill its obligations if we desire to have the whole person in focus. The old position of the "neutral observer" cannot be maintained. The therapist cannot "sit behind his client", he has to "sit beside his client". The therapist has to meet his client "face to face" in an existential relationship between "I" och "Thou", to use Martin Buber's terms. This encounter should not be determined by the therapist's attempt to apply his value system to his client. The correct procedure here must be, that the therapist with great respect for his client, and with warm empathy uses the opportunity to go into the inner world of his client. It is also the obligation of the therapist in certain circumstances to "lend" his value system to the client, and in any case, to let the client use his value system as a reference pattern.

The significance of the therapist's personality in the therapeutic process
We cannot discuss the client's value system and the influence it has upon his life in illness and health, unless we say a word about the therapist's own attitudes, his personality, and value system. It is evident that the therapist's personality is the most decisive factor in the therapeutic process. Why is it that some therapist's attain better results than others, independent of what kind of therapy they make use of? The therapist's personality means more to the outcome of therapy than we will admit, even in client-centered therapy. It is interesting to see that Rogers has paid more attention to this fact in recent years than he did in the beginning. He has relinquished the term "non-directive", and he does not like his previous pictures of the therapist serving as a mirror or a catalyst. He thinks this is far too passive. Rogers thinks of the therapist more in terms of an active co-worker. In his article on "The Therapeutic Relationship: Recent Theory and Research"[6] Rogers states that constructive personality change in the client during psychotherapy is hypothesized as being dependent upon three essential attitudes in the therapist. These attitudes are more important than the therapist's professional qualifications, his therapeutic orientation, or his interview techniques. These attitudes are: congruence or genuineness in the relationship, acceptance or prizing of the client, an accurate empathic understanding of the client's phenomenological world. Rogers even speaks of the therapist showing genuine "non-possessive love" in the therapeutic relation. I cannot see any possibility of doing so unless the therapist's total personality is working in the relationship, even his value system.

What is the real question? In the psychotherapeutic process, these three factors (variables) may be distinguished 1) The personal factors including both therapist and client with their qualifications. 2) The therapeutic climate or contact (relationship). 3) The therapeutic results obtained. It seems clear that the personal factors of the therapist and the client are the basis for both the climate and the result of the therapeuic process. This is the way in which Edwards and Cronbach state it.[7]

We may simplify the problem even more by quoting Jerome D. Frank: "Research in psychotherapy attempts to set up and test hypotheses subsumed under the general question: 'What kinds of therapist activity produce what kinds of change in what kinds of patient? That is, the independent variables lie in the patient's state before the therapist's invention and in the therapist's activity, the dependent variables in changes in the patient's feelings and behavior.'"[8]

No matter how we turn this question around, we come to the conclusion that it is urgent for us to investigate the therapist's work in the therapeutic process.

Edwards and Cronbach say about this: "The most important and unfortunately the least understood situational variable in psychotherapy is the therapist himself. His personality pervades any technique he may use, and because of the patient's dependence on him for help, he may influence the patient through subtle cues of which he may not be aware."[9]

Looking at the therapist as a frame of reference for the client, our first question is: What is it about the therapist that makes the greatest impression upon the client? We will mention three factors: The therapist's education and knowledge, his methods, and his personality. If we should attempt to evaluate what in this connection yields the best results, we could find that opinions are divided. Regularly we adhere to education and methods. Evidently education and methods are of great importance. The guarantee that the whole business does not turn out as quackery lies in the therapist's professional qualifications. This being said, however, our question still stands. We may ask yet a simpler question: Why do some therapists succeed better that others with their clients when they have the same training and use the same methods? Or stated even more intricately: Why do therapists with a poorer education and obviously poorer methods obtain better results than those whose training and methods are scientifically of higher value? We cannot with a smile say that it has always been like that, and the world will always be betrayed. It is of no help to turn to occult phenomena for an explanation either.

We have to draw a very obvious conclusion, that just as there are carpenters, who because of their personal abilities use their tools in a better way than other carpenters, so are there also differences between therapists because of their personal qualifications. What this "ability" consists of is the great question. I have asked myself many times whether it is the twinkle in my eye, or the grasp of my hand, or even the tie I am wearing, or is it my reputation, what other clients have said about me, or my voice, or something mystical that cannot be defined, a kind of nimbus or corona or what? This indeterminable factor that radiates through all I do, perceived consciously or mostly unconsciously by my client, permiates the climate in the therapeutic relationship and establishes the trust which the client has in me. Is this not what really counts? And is this not a reflection of my innermost personality.

Is this not the reason why we as therapists have to go through our own therapy, self-analysis, in order to be in touch with ourselves, to get our own conflicts and feelings under control? Is this not the reason why we proclaim, that as therapists we will not be free from problems and conflicts, but we ought to have them under control?

What personality factors of the therapist enter into the therapeutic process, and which are the most important?

We may answer this question by saying that the client receives a total impression of the therapist. This impression is unanalyzed and cannot easily be demonstrated. One thing is evident, the client is very alert when he comes to his first interview. He has already made up his mind about what he intends to say, what he expects from the interview, and what he thinks of the therapist. Minor things receive more attention than they might deserve. If we have the good fortune to find out what the client thinks of us, either directly from him, or through others, we shall, in most instances, be astonished and surprised. The impression we thought we gave of ourselves, if we gave any attention to it at all, is very seldom congruent with the impression the client had of his therapist. This makes the task of describing this intricate problem, very difficult.

First of all, I think of the voice. My experience is that the therapists who had the greatest success in therapy were people with a warm melodious voice, even with a nimbus of mysticism, which is hard to describe. In all therapeutic practice there is an ingredient of suggestion which is due to the voice of the therapist. Truly the voice is an exponent of the therapist's personality.

Secondly, I think of the therapist's face. His appearance demonstrates more of his personality than he thinks, facial expressions, eyes, smile, and so on. A therapist need not be good-looking, but charm is not unwelcome. However, originality may in some cases balance the lack of charm.

We should never forget the fact that "the eyes are the mirror of the soul".

We give as therapists faint signals which we may call "cues". These "cues" are perceived by the client and given significance far greater than we can imagine. A blink with the eye, a twitch in the face, a gesture with the hand, might give the client information about us which we do not observe. In the warm relationship of therapy, these smaller things are often overdimensioned.

The total pattern of behavior is the photo of our personality. When we think of the identification process and the transference process, it is evident that the therapist's behavior is most important. It is, in any case, evident that the nervous therapist who is manipulating the pencils on his desk, or the therapist who is lazily hanging over his chair will not invite the client to a deeper confidence.

What really concerns us here is what we would call the therapist's "inner attitude", his philosophy of life and his value system. The problem in short is this: Have my personal attitudes toward life, my faith, my philosophy of life, my ethical values, my value systems, anything to do with my work as a therapist? Will it benefit or hurt my client when this comes to the fore? There is no problem when the client's and the therapist's norms are practically the same, but what about when the value systems are opposed to each other?

Two things must be clarified first. One is, that if therapy is to be global, i.e., comprehend the whole person, it is impossible to escape problems of life-view and valuation. Secondly, it is evident that if the therapist wholeheartedly involves himself in his work, he can hardly keep his life-view inside watertight reservoirs.

In order not to be misunderstood, let me say that it is not the obligation of the therapist to inform about life-views, and, by all means, he has to stay away from propagating for his own life-view. This is a task for the minister, the pastoral counselor, and even the philosopher. The therapist has his life-view as a frame of reference for himself and for his client. He can never force his client to accept his life-view. He can only let it, if he is real and transparent, shine through his words and gestures and whole personality. A problem may arise here. How is it possible for the therapist to keep his own life-view intact and still not influence his client to choose this life-view, but leave the client to find his own way? This is a personal question which we have to solve, each of us, for ourselves.

The therapist's world outlook as a point of reference for the client. The therapist's life-view cannot be more than a point of reference for the client. If it is more than that, i.e., the client has a feeling of being forced into the same pattern as the therapist has, then the therapist has transgressed the limits of his profession. On the other hand, the therapist cannot keep his convictions to himself. He is not even supposed to do so.

We have to remember that a life-view is not a rigid and fixed pattern, if so, it does not belong to the integrated area of the person and can serve no growth process for the client. It is of the deepest concern that the therapist keeps his life-view "up-to-date", i.e. it is only the life-view which is in agreement with reality and the level that the therapist has reached in his own personality growth that counts.

We may speak of two extremes when we think of the function of the life-view of the therapist in the therapeutic process. One is the fear that the therapist has of letting his own life-view come to the fore. The reason for this may be that he is not clear himself about his own value system, and as often as he confronts clients' value systems he is initiating conflicts in his own life, conflicts which are not yet solved. Or it may be that the therapist is too anxious to let his life-view shine through, for fear that he might influence his client too much, thus it is better to hide behind a neutral position. On the other hand, the therapist may have a conscious or rather unconscious wish of manipulating his client in the direction of his value system, mostly for his own benefit. This line may lead up to what we may call "brainwashing" and this is not therapy. The therapist has to keep a "via media" where he is concerned not to make too heavy an impact upon the client and still can be calm when he notices that his life-view shines through in the interview. This would all be to the benefit of the client.

The vital point in our discussion here is whether the therapist has a somewhat harmonic (integrated) life-view himself. If he has not, and if he is unable to understand his client's life-view, he will experience negative feelings toward his client and this will call forth mechanisms of defence in him. He feels himself threatened and he has to be "on guard". Sometimes he will feel himself as the "defender of the faith", i.e. his own very dim and indistinct faith, which is not integrated faith. Sometimes he will find himself as a "denier of the faith", both his own and his clients. The one is just as bad as the other.

The therapist must not, on the one hand, run from the life-view "debate" in therapy. On the other hand, he should not initiate it.

Let us have a look at how the client feels and acts, keeping our previous statements in the background. We are not talking here of discussions of life-views. That is not therapy at all and belongs to other fora. We are thinking of the therapist's life-view as a "background" to his personality, not only the open conversation about it, as may occur in therapy.

When the client feels that he touches the life-view of the therapist, he may experience it as a threat or an incitament. In the first place, he may feel that the life-view of the therapist is theatening to him, because it is too idealistic, too high, or it may threaten him because he feels that it is too low, the client has higher ideals than the therapist. In both cases, a fence has been established between the therapist and his client.

It is best when the life-view of the therapist works as an inspiration for the client, an incitament. The life-view of the therapist can, at best, work as a pattern for the client, a pattern which he need to necessarily follow, At best, it may sometimes serve as a pattern with which the client may, if he wishes, correct his own life-view.

A very important point here, is the fact that the therapist by no means has the right to destroy the life-view which the client holds dear to him, even when the therapist thinks that this pattern is working very poorly. My opinion is, that even if the life pattern which my client keeps, has many neurotic trends, the therapist has no right to change it unless the client himself gains insight into his faulty ideals and is willing to change them, with the therapist's help. And one thing more which is important; the life-view of the client should not be built up of material or schedules which the therapist has, but rather according to the often poor material and weak lines which the client himself owns.

Research projects and results on the therapist's role in the therapeutic process.

The therapist's role in therapy has in recent years received considerable attention from Carl R. Rogers. His book "On Becoming a Person" is for the most part, dedicated to the role of the therapist in therapy. Otherwise I agree with Hans H. Strupp when he states that "Research concerned with the therapist's personality and his therapeutic operations is of even more recent origin; indeed, we have scarcely done more than broken the ground for what in future years must become a major research effort."[10]

Let me try to give an overview of what I have found. In the chapter on "Client-centered Therapy in its Context of Research" in "On becoming a Person", Rogers says: "One of the most important characteristics of the client-centered orientation to therapy is that from the first it has not only stimulated research but has existed in a context of research thinking."[11]

Rogers states from his and his students' experiments that "Thus we can say, with some assurance, that a relationship characterized by a high degree of genuineness in the therapist, by a sensitive and accurate empathy on the part of the therapist, by a high degree of regard, respect, liking for the client by the therapist, and by absence of conditionality in this regard, will have a high probability of being an effective therapeutic relationship. These qualities appear to be primary change producing influences on personality and behavior."[12] It is evident that he is speaking of personality traits.

Rogers concludes his chapter on research in psychotherapy after having objected to those who opposed research in such a delicate field as psychotherapy, thinking that this would lead to a depersonalization and change sublime personality dynamics into scientific facts. "Rather the contrary has been true. The more extensive the research the more it has become evident that the significant changes in the client have to do with very subtle and subjective experiences—inner choices, greater oneness within the whole person, a different feeling about one's self. And in the therapist some of the recent studies suggest that a warmly human and genuine therapist, interested only in understanding the moment-by-moment feelings of this person who is coming into being in the relationship with him, is the most effective therapist. Certainly there is nothing to indicate that the coldly intellectual analytical factually-minded therapist is effective. It seems to be one of the paradoxes of psychotherapy that to advance in our understanding of the field the individual must be willing to put his most passionate beliefs and firm convictions to the impersonal test of empirical research; but to be effective as a therapist, he must use his knowledge only to enrich and enlarge his subjective self, and must be that self, freely and without fear, in his relationship to his client."[13]

In his article in Koch's "Psychology: A Study of Science" Rogers describes new areas of research in psychotherapy. Here are the ones he mentions: Perceptual changes during therapy, therapy and learning theory, therapy in relation to humanities and social sciences, therapy and governmental affairs and international relations, therapy and existential philosophy.[14] This last area is of the greatest interest to me.

In two volumes of "Research in Psychotherapy" we shall find valuable material for our purposes.[15] Jerome D. Frank mentions in an article here, "The Role of Cognitions in Illness Healings", that there are three aspects of psychotherapy acting as means of influencing a patient's judgements of himself in the direction of health: The therapist as a socially designed healer, the patient's and the therapist's expectations about treatment, and the effects of the therapist's interpretations on the patient's emotions.[16]

It is evident that Frank puts the greatest emphasis upon the therapist as the most deciding factor in the therapeutic process. He says: "The therapist's social role has two therapeutic aspects: it enhances the patient's expectation of help and conveys to him acceptance of his group."[17]

Daniel J. Levinson writes in, "The Psychotherapist's contribution to the patient's treatment career", that the relatively stable personal-social characteristics of the therapist are these: 1) General level: His "school" of personality theory and therapeutic technique. 2) Individualized level: His conception of the patient, the treatment, and of his own role as therapist. 3) His character traits, values and affective qualities: emotional warmth, tolerance etc. 4) His psycho-social characteristics: His cultural background, religion, political outlook, etc. It is most interesting that these characteristica are the focus of research in therapy.[18]

He who has probably made the keenest observations in our field, is Leonard Krasner. In his chapter on "The Therapist as a Social Reinforcement Machine" he states that "In recent years the therapist has emerged, reluctantly, from the shadow of the patient to a fuller recognition of his behavior in the psychotherapy process."[19] His statement of the therapist as the "social reinforcement machine" is taken from learning theory. He says also that his basic hypotheses are: Psychotherapy is a lawful, predictable, and directive process which can be investigated most parsimoniously within the framework of a reinforcement theory of learning. The variables which affect the therapy process are the same as those in other personal situations which involve the reinforcement, control, manipulation, influencing, or redirection of human behavior.[20]

When Krasner describes the conditions under which the reinforcement procedure is most effective, he names the characteristics of the therapist: 1) Personality, age, appearance, voice, prestige, and socio-economical status. 2) "Placebo" effects. 3) Role taking. He states that the therapist's role taking is dependent upon his values and ethics.

I do not share the viewpoints of Krasner, as his starting point is so different from mine, but I have the deepest respect for his analysis of the problem and his handling of it.

D. Rosenthal takes up the problem of whether the patient's moral value system undergoes change during therapy, and he arrives at the conclusion that patients who have recovered also changed their moral values in the direction of their therapist's.[21]

J.C. Whitehorn says in, "Goals of Psychotherapy", that successful psychotherapy also involves leadership toward preferred values, toward the therapist's conception of what constitutes value in life: "The evidence is strong that the therapist by virtue of his role has the power to influence and control the behavior and values of other human beings. For the therapist not to accept this situation and to be continually unaware of influencing effects of his behavior on his patient would in itself be unethical".[22]

It seems that we are on the right track in the demonstration of our own views, and statements like these can be quoted in abundance. It is a terribly risky task to be a psychotherapist. We are touching the depths of human personality, and we may encroach upon the life of the individual in a decisive way which may mean life or death for the individual. We need to "take our shoes off" and be very careful, knowing what we are doing and doing it in the right way.

Conclusions

As we are going to draw some conclusions as to the influence of the therapist upon his client with reference to his personality, his life-view and value system, we have a feeling of standing at the beginning of a long and troublesome but inspiring road that opens up before us. What we have to say is only tentative.

There are three fields in which we should make our investigations. The first is the fact that the therapist is a *role taker* and a role player in the therapeutic process. This does not mean that there should be something artificial or false in the situation. It is only a fact that we have to admit. The client gives the therapist a role to play, and he himself is playing against this role. This means that we should not think so much in terms of what we are saying and doing, but what we really are in the view of the client, operating as a total individual inside a framework which the client, in his imagination, given to us. We are operating according to the script of the client and the role which he has given to us.

Hjalmar Sundén has devoted his research to the role taking of the human being.[23] Briefly, Sundéns hypothesis is that we are playing roles toward each other and that we often play the other person's role against us. We receive the material for the role function from our perceptions and frames of reference. Religious life is no exception to this rule. Religious experience may, just as all other kinds of experiences, be psychologically ascribed to sense perceptions and frames of reference which have been built upon our perceptions. It is rather easy to see how the value system operates in the role system as a most deciding factor.

These facts may be of interest in the psychotherapeutic process, as the client not only plays his own role, but he permits the therapist to play his, according to a pattern which the client gives to him.

We may draw this conclusion from our thinking. The client cannot really get more out of the therapist than he has presuppositions to invest in him. It is therefore so important for the therapist to "put himself into the client's frame of reference" in order to understand what he is saying and doing, and what he is expecting from the therapist, according to the role the therapist is playing in the imagination of the client. This will, in the last instance, say something about what the therapist means to the client as a person, a total person.

The next field of research is closely connected with what we have said, it concerns the therapist as the client's *alter ego* or image or substitute. A person cannot become himself unless he becomes himself in relation to other (significant) persons in his life. The social perspective comes into focus. If it is to work, the relationship must be positive and accepting. In therapy, it means that the therapist becomes the accepting person that makes it possible for the client to move in the direction of his real self. This takes place through the process of identification. This identification process may take one of two ways: 1) The client identifies himself with the therapist and then the therapist will function as the client's alter ego, which, in the last instance, is the client's own ideal ego. 2) The client identifies the therapist with some "significant other". Then we are operating with an imago or a substitute. This is seen in the transference process.

The therapist may, in the first example, become both what the client admires in himself and what he hates. In all cases, the therapist represents what the client feels as uncompleted in himself. The therapist becomes an ideal, a point of reference, according to which the client may correct his life style and ideals. He is sometimes drawn near to it, and is sometimes repelled by it. In my mind, this therapeutic process has had far too little attention, and we ought to dig deeper here. That is what I have tried to do in this study.

Following Rogers, we may say that here we are dealing with factors that have not been symbolized in the client's self-concept. Significant parts of the perceptual field have been denied admittance to conscious symbolization and acceptance.

The therapist may, in the therapeutic situation, function as a "common denominator" for all that is unfinished in the client. The therapist's task is to help to make the client's alter ego acceptable.

In the second example, the therapist operates as an imago or substitute for someone else. It is not easy to draw lines between the alter ego function and the imago function of the therapist. They mingle with each other. We might say it in this way, that in the alter ego function the unreleased material in the client himself is in focus. In the imago function, the question in focus is the unacceptable aspects of others.

It must be clear, that the therapist's ability to function as an alter ego or imago or substitute depends, when all is said and done, upon his own personality, his age, sex, life attitude, etc.

The third field of investigation is characterized by what we call *transference* problems. Role taking, alter ego, imago, and substitute functions as well as the transference phenomenon, are different sides of one and the same problem: The therapist-client relationship. This relationship is conceived in different ways in different "schools" of therapy. In psychoanalysis the relationship is understood by the transference aspect. The most important task of therapy is to create a relationship that permits the client to give free expression to his feelings in a transference neurosis that has its base in the fact that the therapist is conceived and experienced as an imago. In client-centered therapy, not as much emphasis is placed upon the transference function. This is so for two reasons. First the quality of client-centeredness is at stake when the therapist in the transference situation is conceived as an authority, thus weakening the client's own functions. Secondly, because the therapeutic relationship includes so many other factors and functions that cannot be developed if we onesidedly emphasize the transference function. In client-centered therapy, transference is kept on a minimal level, though we do not neglect the transference phenomenon. The therapist does not consciously create a transference situation, as psychoanalysts do. He will, however, often find himself in a transference situation with his client.

In all these relations we have mentioned, the therapist plays an important role as a reference point for his client. This is really a field of investigation. How the therapist's own personality and his life-view and value system operate in his function as a reference point for his client, is well worth study. What we have done in this study, is a humble attempt to specify the direction in which such investigation might try to find its way.

CHAPTER VIII

Religion, Psychotherapy, and Pastoral Care

Religion and Psychotherapy
Religion and psychotherapy are interested in the integration, growth, and health of the human being, even though this interest is derived from different standpoints. The difference in view exists because the basic aims and methods of the two are distinct. But even if the aims and methods of the one are distinct from those of the other, there ought to be some agreement. Both operate in the same field, both are concerned with dynamic personality processes, and both have, at least partly, the same ends.

Most of the quarrels between psychotherapy and religion are based upon misunderstandings and suspiciousness from both sides. The quarrels frequently result from dogmatic thinking which is not only seen in religion, but in psychoterapeutic theory as well. Some of the bickering has had its grounds in the terminology used, which the other side does not understand or only partly understands.

Religion has been afraid of psychotherapy because of its emphasis upon the horizontal aspect—the immanent and biological. The horizontal aspect of life comprises the problems in human personality which exclude values and the transcendent, the vertical aspects of personality problems. Religion, usually engaged in emphasizing the vertical aspect, frequently feels "out in left field" regarding the horizontal aspect. Psychotherapy, on the other hand, has been suspicious of religion's attempt to help people with personality problems because of its emphasis upon dogma and ethics—the vertical dimension.

The gulf between religion and psychotherapy has, at times been wide and, seemingly, unconquerable. Perhaps the gulf has become a little narrower in our time. This gives hope for the future, even if it does not particularly give promise of agreement in theory. Concurrence, if it were possible, would not be tenable. What can legitimately be hoped for, is that a mutual understanding might be reached which would provide a basis for creative collaboration for the benefit of troubled minds.

The trend in psychological, psychiatric, and psychotherapeutic theory is quite clearly toward the acknowledgment of the contribution of religion in the helping of persons and toward friendship between the two fields. The following are some statements which show this trend or set the stage for it.

Ira Progoff: "Although it began as part of the protest against religion, the net result of modern psychology has been to reaffirm man's experience of himself as a spiritual being."[1]

Progoff says that the change in psychology has been gradual, but it has had a "cumulative effect". "Its net results has been the emergence of a new kind of psychology that no longer seeks to diagnose the modern man and reduce him to 'normality'. It attempts instead to provide a means by which the modern person can experience the larger meanings of life and participate in them with all his faculties. An awareness of man's spiritual nature has gradually replaced the materialism on which psychology was based in its analytical period. Psychology is now prepared to play a new role in Western civilization."[2] The task of psychology is now "to open a road beyond itself, realizing that the creative experiences to which it leads can be *lived only beyond psychology.*[3] ... If psychology is to fulfill the purpose inherent in its historical existence, if it is to enable the modern man to find the meaning of his life, it can do so only by guiding him to an experience that is beyond psychology. This conclusion culminates the analytical phase of depth psychology, and provides the starting point for its growth in new directions."[4] Statements such as Progoffs may prepare a way for a higher estimation of religion in the fields of the therapeutic helping professions.

O. Hobart Mowrer in his attempt to conciliate between psychiatry and religion says, "It seems that the profession of psychiatry is now beginning to think in a new way about the role of religion in mental health and illness,"[5] and he builds his hope upon Viktor Frankl of Vienna, the English psychiatrist Ernest White, and Maves, Galdston, Fromm-Reichmann and Moreno. "Therefore," he continues, "I do not see how we can avoid the conclusion that at this juncture we are in a real crisis with respect to the whole psychotherapeutic enterprise. But I do not think that we are going to remain in this crisis, confused and impotent, indefinitely. There is, I believe, growing realism with regard to the situation on the part of both psychologists and psychiatrists, on the one hand, and ministers, rabbis, and priests, on the other; I am hopeful and even confident that new and better ways of dealing with the situation are in the making."[6] He thinks that Alcoholics Anonymous provides the best preview of things to come.

On the other hand Mowrer castigates religionists; "At the very time that psychologists are becoming distrustful of the sickness approach to personality disturbance and are beginning to look with more benign interest and respect toward certain moral and religious precepts, religionists themselves are being caught up in and bedazzled by the same preposterous system of thought as that from which we psychologists are just recovering."[7] His feeling is that religionists have become too indulgent toward psychology.

A representative of existential analysis, A.J. Ungersma, simply says, "Neurosis can be described as man's progressive self-misunderstanding," and the remedy for this is to help him back again to "the meaning of life." The restoration to mental health "consists in a rebirth of the patient's religious life".[8] and the religious life has also to do with mental health.

We have been arguing for a deeper understanding of theology applied to pastoral counseling. In my opinion the same aspects can be applied to psychotherapy. Then we shall speak of the application of religion to psychotherapy.

Viktor E. Frankl says in the Introduction of his book The Doctor and the Soul: "Man lives in three dimensions: the somatic, the mental, and the spiritual. The spiriual dimension cannot be ignored, for it is what makes us human. To be concerned about the meaning of life is not necessarily a sign of disease or neurosis ... The proper diagnosis can be made only by someone who can see the spiritual side of man."[9]

There is a steadily growing understanding of the importance of applying theology in the counseling process. I would not say that this understanding has always been evident. There is hope for an improved pastoral counseling when theology is not only a fact in the mind of the counselor as a result of his training, but also is actually applied to the counseling procedure. There are some significant signs of this, may we say new, approach. Here is one important statement by Samuel Southard. He gives reasons for the application of theology in the counseling process from the following facts: (1) We have to develop a new understanding of human problems as to their spiritual context. Diagnosis must have spiritual aspects, so ought also the prescriptions which follow the diagnosis. (2) The pastor ought to be more sensitive to the spiritual significance of illness, personal failure, and tragedy. (3) Theology helps to give eternal significance to the common ventures of life. (4) Theology may be used explicitly in the diagnosis of personal problems. (5) A specific theological doctrine may have an obvious and direct relationship to part or the whole of a personal problem. And he continues saying: "When a pastor sees theology and psychology in a vital dialogue and when Christian doctrines spring alive from the face-to-face encounters of counseling, he may have the assurance of a workman who is not ashamed because he rightly handles the word of truth. He has brought the sacred things of God to the human situation of his people with reverence for their personalities and assurance of God's concern."[10]

A book written by Frederic Greeves of Great Britain fell into my hands as I was writing this manuscript. The title is "Theology and the Cure of Souls." He stresses the importance of applying theology in the care of souls, and he does it in a fine and convincing way.[11]

We hope that this book may add something to the understanding that theology is worthy an application by the pastoral counselor, and that he needs to have a clear and distinct theological outlook. One of the main responsibilities of the pastoral counselor is to keep his theological insight intact and to keep pace with new theological thinking. We must, once and for all, do away with the old false concept that theology is dull and sterile and out of date. As far as I know from many years of counseling, there is nothing so helpful in dealing with personality problems than healthy and sound theology. And, by all means, may we do away with the inferiority feeling we developed when we thought that applying the Word of God in the actual problem situation was not as scientific as the application of the most recent findings in psychotherapeutic procedure.

Perhaps this is the crucial point for the future of the pastor's work in counseling. A stronger emphasis upon the Word of God and Christian theology.

The difference between the Continental European view of soul-care and the American aspect of pastoral counseling, is focussed on this point. In the Continental tradition, the emphasis in soul-care has been upon the Bible, the Word of God. Soul-care has been defined by Hans Asmussen as "the proclamation of the Word of God man to man".[12] Eduard Thurneysen states it in a somewhat similar way: "Soul-care occurs in the church as the application of the Word of God to the individual."[13]

This is a far too narrow definition of soul-care. It excludes due consideration of the individual involved and the conditions under which he is living. The Word of God is to be proclaimed without regard to personal needs and personal situation, if we take the definitions for what they are. The individual has to be accommodated to the Word of God. There is really no question of whether the Word of God should fit into the individual's special situation. Bishop Heuch in Norway has written a small book on how to apply soul-care among the sick. Here he says that it is of no use to sprinkle a Word from God here and there as it may occur. He recommends that we "find the key that unlocks the door of the heart".

The Contiental soul-care tradition runs into troubles because of its one-sidedness. The stressing of the Word of God is right, but the neglect of psychological insight and the application of such knowledge is wrong. Thurneysen, being aware of this conflict, tries to get out of this untenable situation by making an artificial division between, what he would call, a "human" *Seelenleitung* (soul-guidance) and the genuine soul-care which is concerned with spiritual factors, which he calls *Seelsorge* (soul care). There are some "human" problems which emerge, but they are not really spiritual in nature, they might even be small problems of daily life. They do not belong to the God-man relationship but more to the man-man relationship. This deep felt problem forces Thurneysen to introduce a breach (ein Bruch) in the soul-care interview in order to cope with "human" problems. Here are his words: "As the soul-care interview is subject to the judgement of the Word of God as concerned with the whole field of human life including all psychological, world view, sociological and moral interpretations and decisions, therefore a breach-line goes through the whole interview, which shows that human decisions and evaluations and the actions taken in accordance with them are by far not irrelevant..."[14]

Thurneysen has run into an unsolvable problem because of his unwillingness to admit that "human" factors also are important parts of the soul-care interview. He tries to solve the problem by stating that there are two levels on which the soul-care interview may take place, the level of the common human life situation and the level of the genuine soul-care situation in which the application of the Word of God is the main point. On the first level, as far as I understand him, we have to use "common sense". But then it is not soul-care in the genuine meaning of that term; it is only soul-guidance. The minister's task is to get his parishioner to leave the level of human affairs and rise to the level of that which is of the uttermost concern, man in his relation to God. This cannot be done without a breach in the interview. The transition from one level to the other is marked by a "breach", both in emphasis and in method.

We may like or dislike this aspect of Christian soul-care. I cannot really find the consistency, but what I admire is the stressing of the sovereignity of the Word of God in soul-care, even at the cost of inconsistency in logic and procedure. This has been the line according to which soul-care in the Lutheran tradition on the Continent has developed, and all honour to the guard of the Word of God.

American soul-care traditions have largely taken the opposite direction. In the American tradition, the emphasis has mainly been laid upon psychiatry, sometimes at the cost of the Word of God, just as the emphasis on the Continent was on the Word of God at the cost of the acceptance and application of new findings of importance for soul-care in psychology and psychotherapy. The Continental tradition in soul-care has made the Bible the one and only textbook. The American tradition has many textbooks in psychiatry beside the Bible, and the Bible has sometimes been set aside. As we look at the training of ministers for their counseling work, we get the impression that they know almost all there is to know about psychotherapy, both in theory and practice. If we consider the clincial training of the minsiters, we get the same impression. And if we think of the vast amount of literature published in this field, we get the same impression again.

It is far from me to criticize this. I ought to be the last one doing so, realizing what it has meant to me to learn, through many visits to America, what it means to have psychological insight into human problems. I just want to state that, the psychotherapeutic view of pastoral counseling might become one-sided if the Word of God is not given its rightful place.

We have to admit that American soul-care traditions have run into some troubles because of a one-sided emphasis upon psychotherapy, and likewise, the European tradition has run into troubles, because of neglect of it.

We must anew remember that soul-care is qualitatively different from psychotherapy even if there are many similarities. Soul-care has its specific perspective: sub specie aeternitatis (under the view of eternity). This perspective is characterized by the Word of God, both as the basis of soul-care and as a means of bringing help to the troubled mind, as well as a goal for man's life.

The problem, of course, is not whether we should apply the Bible and Christian theology or psychological and psychotherapeutic insight to soul-care. It is not a question of either-or; it is question of using them both.

A shift from an all too uncritical application of psychotherapy in pastoral counseling toward a stronger emphasis upon Christian thought is seen in America today, while a greater openness for psychological and psychotherapeutic literature and methods is to be seen in Europe.

Hopefully, there is a basis for co-operation between psychotherapy and religion. Through pastoral care and counseling this co-operation between religion and psychotherapy is made possible. Pastoral counseling is the endeavour on the part of religion to understand psychological dynamics in such a way as to be able to use them meaningfully, along with theological understanding, in the lives of needful persons. Instead of religion being a detrimental force in personality development, it can be a useful factor in personality integration.

Some forms of religion prohibit the healthy development of personality growth. Some present ideas to the religious person which can promote health. A religious form which has become static, can do little of a positive nature to aid personality growth.

Static religion, that is, religion which places great emphasis on doctrines, which utilizes its greatest energies to maintain itself as an institution, which imposes ideas and practices upon the individual that he cannot accept, is detrimental to personality development. Religious ideas which serve only as defense mechanisms and which conceal deep emotional disturbances, are detrimental to personality integration.

Dynamic religion, that is, a religion that takes into account the needs of the person and which meets those needs, religion which is accepted by the individual and has been taken into the service of life, can be used for health and integration by the individual.

Dynamic religion is based upon faith in God as love, positive self-esteem, and a widened life-situation, which derive from trust in God's goodness. Static religion works for the submission of the person under the God of law, with a consequent lowered self-esteem and narrowed life-space. The first kind of religion offers symbols which can work for health while the second tends to result in detriment.

Religion and psychotherapy are not opposites. Some kinds of religion are not therapeutic, and some kinds of therapy are not religious. On the other hand, the Christian religion means to be therapeutic and hopefully accomplishes this end to the glory of God. And hopefully psychotherapy is on the way to accepting religion as something which can be an integrative factor in the health and development of personality.

In order not to be misunderstood the following explanations are in order:

There is no religious psychotherapy. Psychotherapy is treatment of emotional disturbances based upon empirical research and following strictly scientific procedure in the treatment. Psychotherapy has to be placed on the same line as medicine. There is no religious medicine.

On the other hand, psychotherapy which closes its eyes to religious life is not psychotherapy that can be called global, as vital functions in an individual's mental processes are concerned with life-orientation and life-view, and religion seems to have an answer which ought to be heard.

There must be some sort of application of religion in psychotherapy. Perhaps the time has come when religion and psychotherapy, instead of being on a collision course, may feel the obligation and see the mutual help they can render by running together for a while, for the benefit of man.

The details of these new ideas will be discussed later on in this chapter.

The Therapeutic Process

According to an encyclopedia, "Psychotherapy can be defined as the treatment of mental or physical disorder by using mental influences."[15] The different schools of psychiatry, clinical psychology, and psychoanalysis do not agree upon what they think are the causes of the mental or physical disorders, nor the treatment that is most useful. Neither do they agree upon what they think are the criteria of mental health. While there is no unanimity about the process of psychotherapy, we can trace some of the main features of it, upon which most of the psychotherapists would probably agree.

Since disorder consists of a disequilibrium in the mental processes—a distortion of the balance between desires and possibilities, ambivalent feelings, conflicting motives, and so on, the aim of therapy and for all therapists is to restore the inner mental balance.

Futher, as the disorder manifests itself in a blocking of the growth-process or regression to earlier levels of integration, the intention of all psychotherapists is to be instrumental in commencing the growth process again.

Then the agreement between pastoral counseling and psychotherapy usually stops. Within professional counseling circles there is discrepancy as to ideas of origin of disorder. Psychiatrists frequently place emphasis on biological causes, finding the bases for disorder in disturbed metabolism or a strain upon the nervous system or a disturbed inner secretion—which certainly in many cases may be the cause.

In another camp are those who are inclined to place the blame for disorders on broken or poor relationships with other persons. The latter is especially the case among the socio-culturally oriented psychoanalysts. And now there are those who refer the cause of mental disorder to the relationship of the individual to the value-system. One thinks immediately of the existential analysis school and its "search for meaning". It is clear that psychotherapists are increasingly aware of the significance of relationships in the integration and growth and mental health of the human being. As disturbed and broken relationships are the cause of most mental disorders, the purpose of those who can help, is to restore these relationships in the person of the counselor himself.

The relationships which need to be restored are both of an intrapersonal and an interpersonal nature. By intrapersonal relationship, is meant the relationship between contradictory emotions and motives within one individual. Interpersonal relationship refers to the relationships between the individual and his environment.

When the "process" in soul-care is compared with the psychotherapeutic process, we shall find that there are outstanding similarities and differences.

This is my definition of soul care: It is a mental (spiritual) treatment determined by the Word of God, considering the special situation in which the counselee finds himself, with the intention of helping him into a right relationship with God, his fellow man, and himself.[16]

When a person comes to a minister for help, he is troubled by an imbalance within himself. The causes of the imbalance are, according to soul-care theory, broken or poor relationships. The aim of counseling, pastoral and other, is to restore to the individual the ability to build right relationships. So far, one might say that soul-care is a form of psychotherapy.

One could not actually object to this statement. It is, however, important to investigate more in detail the real agreements and disagreements between pastoral counseling and psychotherapy. Let us start with the disagreements.

It is a popular idea that disagreement exists in the use of different language and terminology. Agreement would be obtained if we only agreed upon using the same language. Certainly, theological language and the language used in psychotherapeutic theory and practice are not the same. It might be, however, that even if the terminology is different, the ideas held in both fields are the same.

Let us take one example out of the many. Ministers and psychotherapists are one in the aim of their service—it is to "make a man whole", that is, to be instrumental in restoring him to balance and good relationships. The interpretation of what we mean by "making man whole" differs in psychotherapy and religion. In psychotherapy it means bringing an individual to emotional stability and social adaptability, with man's emotional life and social attitudes uppermost in mind. In religion it also means emotional stability and social adaptability, but it includes another dimension. To be whole for a religious person, also means to be in a right relationship with God. Christian theology holds that, becoming really whole, can only come about when a person arrives at a good relationship with that which is of highest value to him. This means something even beyond his emotional stability and social attitudes, though these will be touched upon at the same time that a person's God-relationship is affected. It can be readily seen that even though the same terminology is used, it does not necessarily mean the same thing. Of what use would it then be to translate theological language into psychotherapeutic language or vice versa?

The aim of therapy is health. The aim of soul-care is salvation. No word would equate the two concepts. The highest goal we can try for, speaking of terminology, is a mutual understanding of one another's terminology, the acceptance of the other's terminology, and willingness to cooperate in a purposeful way.

The difference between psychotherapy and soul-care is qualitative, not semantical. Soul-care is, first and foremost, concerned with the vertical dimension of the dynamic field of integration—the value system, God. In this dimension life finds meaning and goal; this is the basis for healthy personality integration. In this dimension, one views life *sub specie aeternitatis*, under the view of eternity. This means that religious growth is nurtured by soul-care.

Psychotherapy is mainly concerned with the horizontal dimension of life, which means that it takes interest in the individual and his environment, focussing upon the dynamics of the relationships on a genuine "human" level.

Following is a diagram which tries to pinpoint and clarify the similarities and distinctions between psychotherapy and soul-care.

COMPARISON OF PSYCHIATRI, PSYCHOTHERAPY, AND PASTORAL COUNSELING

I. BASIS

	Common field	Special field
Psychiatry		Knowledge of man acquired through scientifically accepted methods: Observation. Experiment. Empirical procedure.
Psychotherapy		
Pastoral Counseling	Knowledge of man.	Knowledge of man based upon Revelation through the Word of God and through Christian experience. A priori et posteriori.

II. Operational field

	Common field	Special field
Psychiatry		Mental disorder, organic, constitutional and functional.
Psychotherapy	Man as a psychosomatic entity.	Functional mental disorders.
Pastoral Counseling		Mental disorders of spiritual and ethical nature (sin).

III. Ethiology

	Common field	Special field
Psychiatry		Disturbance in organic, physiological balance—metabolism and glandular disturbance.
Psychotherapy	Mental harmony, the balance between intra-psychical relationships.	The mental (and organic) balanced disturbed. Psychodynamisms.
Pastoral Counseling		Disturbances of spiritual balance. Maladjustment toward God, man and self (sin).

IV. Diagnostic methods

	Common field	Special field
Psychiatry		Neurological and glandular examination, metabolism tests, narco-analysis.
Psychotherapy	Biographical data; personal relations and milieu-factors; impressions from personal behavior—body, speech, gestures, etc.; interviews.	Tests, "Einfalls" technique, dreams, hypnosis, interview.
Pastoral Counseling		Confrontation with the Word of God, confession, relationship.

V. Therapy

	Common field	Special field
Psychiatry		Medical treatment: injections, vitamin treatment, shock treatment, chemical treatment, surgery.
Psychotherapy	Psycho-therapy: Mental influence through verbal and other means, interviews; Catharsis.	Hypnosis, suggestion, "Einfalls" technique, dreams.
Pastoral Counseling		The Word of God, prayer, meditation, confession with absolution.

VI. Intention (aim)

	Common field	Special field
Psychiatry	To help the entire man toward integration, helping get rid of disturbing factors, helping man to grow and meet life in a mature way, and helping him form healthful relationships, with his environment.	Health, Emphasis upon intrapersonal relations.
Psychotherapy		Health. Emphasis upon interpersonal relations.
Pastoral Counseling		Salvation. Emphasis upon extra-personal relations (relation to God).

The qualitative differences between soul-care and psychotherapy are found mainly in the basis for their respective understanding of man. The basis for soul-care's understanding of man is the Bible, the source *par excellence* of knowledge about the nature of man. The basis for psychotherapy's understanding is the scientific knowledge of man. This does not mean that soul-care is not interested in the scientific knowledge of man—on the contrary, it avails itself of scientific findings—but it is centrally interested in the biblical interpretation of him. Part of the purpose of these writings is to show that science has much to contribute to the pastor's knowledge of man. As far as I can see, there is no essential disagreement between the knowledge of man in the Bible and that in science. Insight into the human personality which the sciences have now given, in some senses, is far greater now than it was when the Bible was composed. The Bible is the *basis* for soul-care but science provides some of the *means*. In caring for persons and working with them, the minister does not oppose what has been done in science, but uses the understanding of human and divine personality witnessed to in the Bible.

The hope of soul-care is man's salvation; the hope of psychotherapy is the restoration of man's health. Soul-care is certainly interested in the health of the individual—health is integrally related to his self-concept and God-concept; everything that concerns man, concerns soul-care; but the endeavor of soul-care is to bring man into a strengthened relationship with God, his Father. Soul-Care is a therapy *sub specie aeternitatis*, under the view of eternity. It takes the vertical dimension of men's lives in deepest earnest. A person's relationship to God is the most vital point for his health.

The agreements are found in the *methods* used, the means of diagnosis and therapy. Soul-care makes use of psychotherapeutic means which are helpful and in accord with the basis and the intention of soul-care.

Religion As a Therapeutic Agency
Let us emphasize our point that healthy forms of religion are not detrimental to personality, to personality growth, and integration. "Healthy" means that which promotes health. In speaking of "healthy religion" we mean religion based upon the theological interpretation of the New Testament.

The attacks against religion as an undermining agency of an individual's mental health, may be merited in the case of some forms of religion, but there are no grounds for attacking all religion as unhealthy. The Christian religion, when rightly interpreted and rightly applied, does not oppose the mental and physical health of the person. It holds out to him elements of support and help. When religion is spoken of in the following pages, it refers to this sort of religion.

If religion is a prophylactic agency in personality, what are its claims? Does religion prevent disturbing influences from attacking personality? Is religion a medium in which personality growth and development can take place?

It is not realistic to hope that anything in this world of discomfort and struggle would be able to dispel all disturbing influences upon personality. Religion does not shield us against attack, but it gives us a means of bearing up under it and conquering it is devastation. That is all we can ask for. To be protected from every storm in life is to be deprived of the possibility of growth. Religion may even be the source of storm as it confronts us with the call to use our lives purposefully, bringing us into a knowledge of God's demands upon our life. This confrontation may be in the form of the crisis experiences discussed earlier. Relationship with God through His Church offers a way out of crisis. It invites release from the guilt and negative self-feelings through reconciliation and love in the person of Jesus Christ.

Christian faith provides fertile soil in which personality may flourish. It offers man a *conceptual* world in which there is unity and meaning, and it offers man a *dynamic* world in which there is power to live—it offers life, and that, abundantly. Meaning and life are requisite for existence. Who would care to exist without some meaning and promise to life?

Religious or theological concepts are of the greatest importance for the well-being of the human being. "Religion is an essential aspect of mature personality," Gordon Allports says, "because it enables man to discover a fundamental value underlying all thing and therefore gives him a unifying perspective."[17]

Jung tells us, "During the past thirty years, people from all the civilized countries of the earth have consulted me. I have treated many hundreds of patients, the larger number being Protestants, a smaller number Jews, and not more than five or six believing Catholics. Among all my patients in the second half of life—that is to say, over thirty-five—there has not been one whose problem in the last resort was not that of finding a religious outlook on life. It is safe to say that every one of them fell ill because he had lost that which the living religions of every age have given to their followers, and none of them has been really healed who did not regain his religious outlook . . . It seems to me that side by side with the decline of religious life the neuroses grow noticeably more frequent . . . Every one of them (modern man and woman) has the feeling that our religious truths have somehow or other grown empty."[18]

When one loses his feeling of purpose and moral demand through drifting away from religion, he is faced with meaninglessness. Paul Tillich says that, "The anxiety of meaninglessness is anxiety about the loss of an ultimate concern, of a meaning which gives meaning to all meanings. This anxiety is aroused by the loss of a spiritual center, of an answer, however symbolic and indirect, to the question of the meaning of existence."[19]

Religion offers a meaning in life. "A man's religion is the audacious bid he makes to bind himself to creation and to the Creator," Allport points out. "It is the ultimate attempt to enlarge and to complete his own personality by finding the supreme context in which he rightly belongs."[20]

If a man does not succeed in obtaining meaning in life, he actually has no *raison d'etre*, no reason for being. Mental disorders are, more often than is realized, the effect of this lack of meaning in life. Jung tells us, "About one third of my cases are not suffering from any clinically definable neurosis, but from the senselessness and aimlessness of their lives. I should not object if this were called the general neurosis of our time."[21] Anton Boisen affirms this: "To be at one with that which is supreme in our hierarchy of loyalties, that to which men generally give the name God, is ever essential to mental health."[22]

The contribution of Viktor E. Frankl, concerning this important fact of gaining and supporting meaning in life, is of the greatest importance. He states that the time is not up for a "psychotherapy in terms of the mind", and he says that this kind of psychotherapy "is specifically designed to handle those sufferings over the philosophical problems with which life confronts human beings."[23]

These quotes from outstanding men in philosophy and psychotherapy illustrate the importance of making known the right theological concepts. The task of the church, the school, and the home, in religious education and in imparting the correct and healing knowledge about God, cannot be underestimated. Here is where one learns of relationship, acceptance and meaning. Here is where one's relationships with God, with oneself, and with others are established and nurtured.

In the warmth of the religious fellowship of the church, personality finds opportunity for growth, and dynamic power for coming to grips with problems and realizing the possibilities for personal development. This dynamic power has its source in the love of God through Jesus Christ and, in one respect, is redemptive and forgives sin, and in the other respect, is educative, guiding and giving strength through the Holy Spirit.

Religion In the Therapeutic Process

The help offered in the therapeutic process depends to a large extent upon the therapist's or counselor's insight into the causes of the counselee's problems, and his knowledge of personality dynamics. With these as his equipment, he can help the person with problems through a therapeutic relationship with him; together the two of them work for a creative relationship in which understanding comes. The main thrust of this volume is to show the importance of sharp insight into the functioning of personality dynamics, in order to be of service in the counseling relationship. Diagnosis is an important part of therapy.

These are questions which must be put to religion concerning its therapeutic value: Can elements of religion help to bring insight into personality problems? How can religious ideas provide a basis for the reconstruction of a personality? Does religion offer any remedy to build up what has been broken down in a personality? If so, are they equally relevant for psychotherapy?

A. Meader shares this experience; "My consultations have convinced me that a one-sided scientific attitude is not sufficient to give the patient the best help, the help he expects and wants... It is important for physicians, and particularly us psychotherapists, to recognize how pastoral care might produce soothing, enlightening and strengthening results even in serious physical and mental suffering... Other tools and methods might be found than those which have been accorded to us doctors, a method *sui generis* that has its complete application outside our work as doctors. This means a need for not only widening our knowledge, but gives us further basis for tolerance and willingness to co-operate with ministers."[24] And Wise says, "Counseling is fundamentally a religious process."[25]

The insight into personality problems which the Bible contains is great. It represents the gathering of knowledge about man through ages, not only in his "religious setting", but in every setting of life. As one reads the Bible, he is struck by the perceptiveness and understanding of psychological dynamics found in it. It is a misfortune that the knowledge of humanity which the Bible has, is so little known and so poorly applied.

A large body of literature of the Christian Church gives us knowledge of the experience of Christian men through autobiographies, confessions, and devotional literature. If all this is added to the biblical knowledge of man, we have an abundance of material giving us insight into the human heart. It has value for those who would help others in times of personal need. It demonstrates the innermost feelings and yearnings of people. This material adds to our knowledge of man, and what external and internal factors combined to make those lives meaningful in history. For instance, Jeremiah's introspections and lamentations and Augustine's *Confessions* give us pictures of what went on in their thoughts and feelings, especially as they sought to do God's will in the social context in which they found themselves.

People continue to have valid religious experiences. The men of old were not alone in experiencing a relationship with God. Experimental studies can be made today of religious experience, as psychologically verifiable as other fields of human experience. The research and literature on the practice of pastoral counseling and soul-care has increased in volume and depth of understanding. As for the disturbed emotional state in personality disorder, what sort of solution does Christian theology offer? In countless references, the Bible promises rest and peace and comfort and courage. It offers these things to the extent that it can be said that, this is the content of the Bible message, especially the New Testament message. The basis for this reconstruction of the inner balance of the mind is the grace of God.

Let us ask how this works in times of stress and trial. How does one face tragedy and disaster in life? No man can avoid tragedy and suffering and sorrow. Most people have a pattern of life that suits the sunny days. When days of tragedy come, it leaves most of us in despair. Job's predicament was not his tragedy, but the way in which he faced it. His friends had only inadequate and false answers to his problem. They thought that the only reason for the misfortune must be found in some wrongdoings in Job's life.

Meaning in tragedy is more difficult to find than anything else in our lives. There is no other situation in history in which tragedy has served a greater purpose in such a convincing way as was done with the cross of Jesus.

Evidently, there are answers to be found to tragedy outside religion. The value of religion, however, cannot be questioned. I remember one bitterly cold Sunday in February 1942 when a big crowd was gathered outside the Cathedral of Trondheim in Norway. The nazies had blocked the doors of the church in order that no one should enter the sanctuary where the dean of the Cathedral was conducting the services in opposition to the command of the nazi-regime. Despair and hatred could be seen in the faces of the big crowd. Then suddenly some started to sing: "A mighty fortress is our God". The singing spread throughout the whole crowd. Everybody took part in the singing. Peace and confidence marked the faces, and as one of the clergy encouraged people to go home quietly, not giving way to demonstrations, people went calmly to their homes. We had our service outside the church, singing one single hymn. That made the difference in the attitude of the people.

I would not like to use the phrase, that religion soothes the mind in times of tragedy. I would rather say that religion gives meaning to tragedy and power to overcome it. It is sufficient to refer to the concentration camps during the Second World War. The prisoners had less of everything except religion in the concentration camps; and religion gave that peace of mind that could face and conquer tragedy.

Perhaps the generations before us were better off than we are. They had more religion and less comfort. We have less religion and more comfort. Comfort does not conquer tragedy, but religion does.

Face to face with personal failures, shortcomings and sin, religion can and does offer understanding, love and a new basis for life. Certainly, if a person has a well founded philosophy of life, even if this philosophy does not have much to do with religion, this will be of help to him. Every value system, religious or not, has that influence upon personality. Still it is uncontradicted that religion, we are here as elsewhere speaking of the Christian religion, has something to offer those who do not succeed in the hard combat of life. The New Testament, as well as the Old gives evidence of that. Most outstanding in this respect are the parables of Jesus about the prodigal son and the good samaritan.

Man may sink into the abyss of despair, but if there is a glimpse of religion in the pit of despair, he is not without hope.

In the face of death, man's poise and power diminish. The thought of nonbeing to use Paul Tillich's terms, is dreadful, but there is a power to resist death in religion.

Viktor Frankl says, that death is meaningful in itself because death puts a stop-signal in our lives. Death is a sign of our finitude. If death did not put that end to our lives, life would become meaningless because we would not have any responsibility, as we might postpone all our doings indefinitely. We should have sufficient time. "Finality," he says, "temporarily, is therefore not only an essential characteristic of human life, but also a real factor in its meaningfulness."[26]

This is good for intellectually trained minds, for those who can dig into and make use of such philosophy. In my opinion, it is a little too sophisticated for common people. Common people wish for a simpler answer to their need of overcoming death. Man's natural need confronting death is a wish to live, and the longer life, the better, is the most common view. The Old Testament's evidence of a blessing from God, was a long life and a fertile procreation. In primitive thinking, the prolonging of life is thought of as a life continuing through the offspring, and this gave comfort, particularly because primitive man felt himself part of a whole, the tribe or the clan.

In our days, however, and in our western civilization with emphasis upon individuality, it is hard for man to face death. He feels that death is the annihilation of individual life, and that he cannot stand. The overcoming of dread for death must be a question of the value system a person has developed in his life. As the value system is working in life, as we have tried to demonstrate, it also works confronting death. It is a question of faith when man is facing death, and faith is the value system in action.

What basis is there in the Christian religion for a reconstruction of broken relationships with others? Self-understanding leads to the understanding of others. Self-acceptance leads to the acceptance of others. When one experiences being accepted by God, he is lead both to self-acceptance and acceptance of his fellow man. Through man's experience of grace he is enabled to forgive those who trespass against him, fulfilling the commandment to forgive. Faith and love is the Christian value system in action, which forms the core of personality integration.

The Christian religion offers a value system, a Person who gives meaning to life, a new life. The meaning of a life cannot be separated from a man's God and his religion. Any meaning of life or interpretation of life without the religious aspect is only a partial meaning. It can never cover the whole world in which we live unless it comprehends God.

Through finding this meaning and goal for one's life, through the Christian faith, one has found the possibility of a new faith and confidence in oneself. To have a conviction of being in accord with one's Creator and of being led by His providence, supports one's self-concept and self-confidence.

The hope of healthy religion is to cleanse the self-concept, making it more in accordance with reality and promoting the healthy self-concept as the religious person finds new life.

To have faith means to have faith in the life-situation. Religion in and of itself, is not detrimental to the life-situation, except where the life-situation is detrimental to the individual. The Christian faith does not require anything that would not be in our best interest. When it is thought, and it is sometimes mistakenly believed, that we should sacrifice merely for the sake of the sacrifice, it is a misinterpretation of the Christian idea, for sacrifice in the Christian sense is the giving of ourselves in God's service in order, not to be destroyed, but to be restored.[27]

In order to cooperate with the integration of the whole personality, the life situation needs to be submitted to the value-system of the individual. Then he is free of petty rule-keeping and worry about decisions.

The means for building up broken relationships is, in the Christian religion, *love*. Bonthius thinks that the contribution of religion to man's mental health is, "Knowledge of God's mighty and eternal love for them, and opportunity to respond personally to that love with all they have."[28]

What relevance has all this for psychotherapy? According to Wise, the task of psychotherapy is "to discover anew the meaning of life, . . . embody the meaning in symbols that may be intelligible and meaningful to modern man, and . . . develop techniques capable of transforming personality and of leading men out of the night and into the day."²⁹ If this is true, and we think it is, then religion has a real contribution to make to psychotherapy. Religion offers meaning in life. In psychotherapeutic theory and practice, the need for purpose and meaning has come more and more into focus. The necessity of rethinking the basic needs of man is recognized on every hand. Freud thought that man's basic need was the search for pleasure. Adler thought it was the search for power. The cultural psychoanalysts thought that man's striving for cultural and social acceptance was the basic need. Existential analysis thinks that man's deepest need is the search for meaning.

The emphasis of therapeutic theory is upon an interpretation of life's struggles and problems, which is in accord with the thrust of pastoral care. In the latter, the emphasis is laid upon the value system. This religious aspect, the offering of meaning in life, should not pervade the whole area of psychotherapy, but it seems right that it should supplement it. There are biological causes of mental disorders which must be handled on the biological level. But there is also a level of life-orientation which causes mental stress and disorder. These life-orientation questions need to be coped with on their own level. A failure in psychotherapy has been an unwillingness to see and admit to the life-orientation problems in the sufferings of the human spirit. And this is where religious counseling can best work. If the one works with the other, together they can offer hope and greater help to troubled people.

Co-operation Between Religion and Psychotherapy
The need for co-operation between religion and psychotherapy is stated by Mowrer. "What can be done to stem the rising tide of mental disorder in our time? Historically, medicine and religion have failed to give the answer—medicine because of its biological biases, religion because of its otherworldly, mystical biases. Yet between the two of them, medicine and religion seem to come close to encompassing the whole truth. Perhaps we can say that each of them contains half the truth: the modern medical approach is right in that it is scientific, naturalistic, empirical, and religion is right in its contention that the problem of personal happiness and normality is inextricably bound up with the moral nature of man. Perhaps it is not too gross an oversimplification to suggest that our best hopes for improved happiness and better mental health lie in a new direction of *a new* discipline, one that will combine a concern for *both* empiricism and ethics. If only the world can hold together politically for another generation, I think we will see very significant progress made along these lines."³⁰

We can at least agree with Mowrer's intentions, if not in detail with what he has said. It is not completely right to say that medicine and religion contain half the truth. We think it is better to say that both contain the truth, but it is not quite the same truth, or better yet, it is practically the same truth seen from different angles. In order to be of service to persons, we should try to understand both kinds of truth; they are not contradictory.

It is not even necessary to invent a new discipline, either. It is much simpler than that. It suffices when the medical doctor admits that the human being is not only flesh and blood but a spiritual being as well and when the religious worker "admits a bit more flesh" in his theories.

Historically there was no breach between medicine and religion. The priest was the medical man. The division between medicine and religion came about when medicine could not tolerate mysticism any longer and became a natural science. Once the cleavage was made, the gulf became larger and larger.

A reunion between the two is unlikely and unfeasible. Their respective methods, interest, and problems are far too different.

Some of the things toward which psychiatrists and ministers might work for the improvement of their service to needful persons are:

1. Greater understanding of one another's profession, problems, methods, and interests.
2. Increased acceptance of one another's service to the troubled person.
3. More cooperation within the field in which the two professions meet as they help men in mental need.

These do not purport to a merging of the two professions. Each group has its own legitimate needs to serve, which would not be covered if the members of the one diluted their efforts by dabbling in the other. Soul-care is not psychotherapy in its narrow meaning, and neither is the psychotherapist a soul-shepherd in the sense that the minister is.

It is important, since each have their field of specialty, that the one refer patients to the other as the case may call for referral. The minister should at least know enough about emotional problems to be able to distinguish that mental need which he is unable to meet, and refer it to the psychiatrist. The psychiatrist ought to be able to distinguish a theological deficiency in a patient and be humble enough to refer it to the minister if he is not equipped to handle it himself.

There is danger involved if members of the professions are unwilling to cooperate. The minister is not qualified nor able to take on cases of mental disorder, either wittingly or unwittingly. He needs to know the difference between temporary problems of a largely healthy person, and psycho-neurosis, and psychosis, for his own protection as well as for the maximim benefit of the counselee. There have been numerous cases where a minister has got himself into serious difficulty through attempting to help persons with problems beyond his ken. On the other hand, a psychiatrist can help a person work through his problems and help him set goals for himself but he cannot give him ultimate meaning and purpose. A professional therapist can only help with human problems in a man-to-man relationship, he cannot really offer him a human-God relationship or an ultimate hope.

Notes

Chapter I
1 Murphy, Gardner: Personality, p. 66.
2 Angyal, Andras: Foundations for a Science of Personality, p. 299.
3 Oates, Wayne E.: The Religious Dimensions of Personality, p. 209.
4 Rommetveit, Ragnar: Ego i moderne psykologi, p. 16.
5 Ibid. p. 25.
6 Ibid. p. 55.
7 Ibid. p. 69.
8 Erikson, Erik H.: Childhood and Society, p. 239.
9 Rogers, Carl R.: Clientcentered Therapy, p. 532.
10 Ibid. p. 500.
11 Ibid. pp. 522—523.
12 Ibid. p. 523.
13 Ibid. p. 524.

Chapter II
1 Maslow, A.H.: New Knowledge in Human Values, p. 13.
2 Ibid. p. 14.
3 Ibid. p. 39.
4 Ibid. p. 39.
5 Ibid. p. 38.
6 Frankl, Viktor E.: The Doctor and the Soul, p. XII.
7 Frankl, Viktor E.: Theorie und Therapie der Neurosen.
8 Maslow, A.H.: Op. cit.
9 Bühler, Charlotte: Values in Psychotherapy.
10 Harper, Robert H.: Psychoanalysis and Psychotherapy, p. 156.
11 Patterson, C.H.: Counseling and Psychotherapy.
12 Rogers, Carl R.: Clientcentered Therapy, p. 149.
13 Ibid. p. 150.
14 Ibid. p. 292.
15 Hart, J.H. & Tomlinson, T.M.: New Directions in Clientcentered Therapy, p. 427.
16 Ibid. p. 428.
17 Ibid. p. 410.
18 Nilsen, E. Anker: M.A. Thesis: The Idea of God and Self-evaluation and Doctor's dissertation: The Idea of God and Personality Integration.
19 Otto, Rudolf: The Idea of the Holy, pp. 12—13.
20 Tillich, Paul: Systematic Theology, Vol. I, p. 217.
21 Newman, Francis W.: The Soul. Its Sorrows and its Aspiration. Quotted from William James: Religious Experience.
22 Rogers, Carl R.: Toward a Modern Approach to Values, p. 161.
23 Ibid. p. 163.
24 Ibid. p. 163.
25 Ibid. p. 163.
26 Ibid. p. 163.
27 Ibid. p. 166.
28 Bühler, Charlotte: Values in Psychotherapy.
29 Ibid.
30 Erikson, Erik H.: Identity and the Life Cycle.
31 Erikson, Erik H.: Identity and the Life Cycle.

32 Maslow, A.H.: Op.cit. p. 38.
33 Maslow, A.H.: Motivation, p. 66.
34 Ibid. p. 89.
35 Ibid. p. 91.
36 Madsen, K.B.: Moderne psykologiske teorier, p. 80.
37 Maslow, A.H.: New Knowledge. Op.cit. p. 123.
38 Ibid. p. 128.
39 Ibid. p. 151.
40 Ibid. pp. 152—153.
41 Ibid. p. 151.
42 Ibid. p. 178.
43 Ibid. p. 179.
44 Ibid. p. 200.
45 Ibid. p. 195.
46 Angyal, Andras: Op.cit. p. 172.
47 Rogers, Carl R.: Clientcentered Psychotherapy, pp. 19—20.
48 Matt. 5, 27—28.
49 Mark. 2, 27.
50 Rogers, Carl R.: On Becoming a Person, p. 163.
51 Maslow, A.H.: Op.cit. p. 183.

Chapter III

1 Young, P.T.: Emotion in Man and Animal, pp. 357—358.
2 Chisholm, G.B.: The Reestablishment of Peacetime Society, Psychiatry, Vol. IX, 1946, p. 6.

Chapter IV

1 Rommetveit, Ragnar: Op.cit. p. 25.
2 Lecky, Prescott: Selfconsistency, p. 3.
3 Ungersma, A.J.: The Search for Meaning, p. 62.
4 Symonds, Percival M.: Dynamic Psychology, pp. 361 ff.
5 Symonds, Percival M.: The Ego and the Self, p. VI.
6 Symonds, Percival M.: Dynamic Psychology, p. 371.
7 Young, Kimball: Personality and Problems of Adjustment, p. 164.
8 Mead, George H.: Mind, Self, and Society, p. 135.
9 Horney, Karen: Self-analysis, p. 63.
10 Angyal, Andras: Op.cit. pp. 179 ff.
11 May, Rollo: The Meaning of Anxiety, p. 6
12 Symonds, Percival: The Ego and the Self, p. 81.
13 Ibid. p. 82.
14 Ibid. p. 89.
15 Kaila, Eino: Personlighetens psykologi, p. 204.
16 Cameron, Norman, and Ann, Margaret: Behavior Pathology, p. 99.
17 Sullivan, Harry Stack: Conceptions of Modern Psychiatry, Journal of the Biology and Pathology of Interpersonal Relations, Vol. I 1940 p. 7.
18 Fromm, Erich: Selfishness and Self-love, Psychiatry Vol. II, 1939, p. 513.

Chapter V

1 Coe, George Albert: The Psychology of Religion, p. 60.
2 James William: The Varieties of Religious Experience, p. 26.
3 Ibid. p. 53.
4 Nevius, Warren Nelson: Religion as Experience and Thruth, p. 42.
5 Coe: Op.cit. p. 61.
6 James, William: Op.cit. pp. 88 ff.
7 Hjalmar Sundén: Religionen och rollerna, p. 47.
8 Ibid. p. 9.
9 Ibid. p. 53.

10 Schjelderup, Harald und Kristian: Über drei Haupttäpen der Religiösen Erlebnisformen und ihre Psychologishe Grundlage.
11 E. Anker Nilsen: The Idea of God and Personality Integration.
12 James, William: Op.cit., p. 166.
13 Källstad, Thorvald: John Wesley and the Bible, p. 36.
14 Ibid. p. 36.
15 Ibid. p. 237.
16 Ibid. p. 237.
17 Ibid. pp. 238 ff.
18 Murphy: Op.cit., p. 553.
19 Mowrer, O. Hobart: Learning Theory and Personality Dynamics, p. 518.
20 Wise, Carroll A.: Religion in Illness and Health, p. 122.
21 Rogers, Carl R.: Counseling aand Psychotherapy, pp. 217 ff.
22 Murphy: Op.cit., p. 642.
23 Symonds, Percival M.: Dynamic Psychology, pp. 274 ff.
24 Bonthius, Robert H.: Christian Paths to Self-Acceptance, p. 178.
25 Mowrer: Learning Theory and Personality Dynamics, p. 462.
26 Hollingworth, H. L.: Psychology and Ethics, p. 275.
27 Mowrer: Op. cit., p. 462.
28 Höffding, Harald: Oplevelse og Tydning, p. 25.
29 Braaten, Leif S.: The Movement from Non-Self to Self in Client-centered Psychotherapy, J. Couns. Psychol., 8, 20—24.
30 Wise, Carrol A.: Pastoral Counseling, pp. 162 ff.
31 Hebr. XI, 1.
32 Pratt: Op.cit., pp. 35 ff.
33 Fromm, Erich: Selfishness and Self-Love. Psychiatry, Vol. II, 1949, p. 513.
34 Wise: Op.cit., p. 144.
35 Ibid. p. 213.
36 Ibid. p. 150.

Chapter VII

1 Rogers, Carl R.: Toward a Modern Approach to Values, p. 160.
2 Ibid. p. 160.
3 Ibid. p. 160.
4 Ibid. p. 167.
5 Nilsen, E. Anker: The Idea of God and Personality Integration.
6 Rogers Carl R.: The Therapeutic Relationship. Recent Theory and Research, Australian Journal of Psychology Vol. 17, 1965, no. 2, pp. 95—108.
7 Rubinstein, Eli A. and Parloff, Morris B.: Research in Therapy, Vol.I, 1959.
8 Op. cit. p. 10.
9 Op. cit. p. 17.
10 Rubinstein and Parloff: Research in Psychotherapy, Op. cit. p. 25.
11 Rogers, Carl R.: On Becoming a Person, p. 244.
12 Ibid. p. 265.
13 Ibid. p. 269.
14 Koch, S. (Ed.) Psychology: A Study of Science, Vol. II, Formulations of the Person in the Social Context, 1959, pp. 184—256.
15 Rubinstein, Eli A. and Parloff, M.: Research in Psychotherapy Vol. I 1959 and Strupp, H.H. and Luborsky Vol. II, 1962.
16 Rubinstein and Parloff. Op. cit. p. 5.
17 Ibid. p. 5.
18 Ibid.
19 Ibid. p. 60.
20 Ibid. p. 61.
21 Rosental, D.: Changes in some Moral Values following Psychotherapy. Journal of Consulting Psychology, 1955, Vol. 19, pp. 431—436.
22 Rubinstein & Parloff. Op.cit. p. 69.
23 Sundén, Hjalmar: Religionen och rollerna.

Chapter VIII

1. Progroff, Ira: The Death and Rebirth of Psychology p. 3.
2. Ibid. p. 254.
3. Ibid. p. 255.
4. Ibid. p. 259.
5. Mowrer, O. Hobart: The Crisis in Psychiatry and Religion. p. 4.
6. Ibid. p. 45—46.
7. Ibid. p. 52.
8. Ungersma, A.J.: The search for Meaning. p. 11.
9. Frankl, Viktor E.: The Doctor and the Soul. p. IX.
10. Oates, Wayne E.: An Introduction to Pastoral Counseling. pp. 243—250.
11. Greeves, Frederic: Theology and the Cure of Souls.
12. Asmussen, Hans: Die Seelsorge. p. 15.
13. Thurneysen, Eduard: Die Lehre von der Seelsorge. p. 19.
14. Ibid. p. 114.
15. Harriman, Philip Lawrence: The Encoclypedia of Psychology. p. 823.
16. Nilsen, E. Anker: Nye veier i sjelesorgen. p. 166.
17. Allport, Gordon W.: The Individual and his Religion. p. 226.
18. Jung, C.G.: Modern Man in Search of a Soul. pp. 264, 266, 268.
19. Tillich, Paul: The Courage to be. p. 47.
20. Allport, Gordon W.: The Individual and his Religion. p. 142.
21. Jung, C.G.: The Practice of Psychotherapy. p. 41.
22. Boisen, Anton T.: The Exploration of the inner World. p. 173.
23. Frankl, Viktor E.: The Doctor and the Soul. p. 33.
24. Maeder, A.: Veien til sjelelig sunnhet. pp. 148 and 153.
25. Wise, Carrol A.: Pastoral Counseling. p. 145.
26. Frankl, Viktor E.: Op. cit. p. 73.
27. Romans 12, 1.
28. Bonthius, Robert H.: Christian Paths to Self-Acceptance. p. 200.
29. Wise, Carrol A.: Religion in Illness and Health. p. 204.
30. Mowrer, O. Hobart: Learning Theory and Personality Dynamics. p. 570.

Bibliography

Adler, Alfred: Praxis und Theorie der Individualpsychologie. München: J.F. Bergmann, 1924.
Alexander, Franz: Fundamentals of Psychoanalysis. New York: W.W. Norton & Co., Inc. 1948.
Alexander F. and French: Psychoanalytic Theory. New York: Ronald Press. 1946.
Allan, D. Maurice: The Realm of Personality, New York: Abingdon Cokesbury Press. 1947.
Allport, Gordon W.: Personality. New York: Henry Holt and Co. 1937.
—, The Individual and his Religion. New York: The Macmillan Co., 1950.
—, Becoming. Basic considerations for a Psychology of Personality. New Haven: Yale University Press. 1955.
Angyal, Andras: Foundations for a Science of Personality. New York: The Commonwealth Fund. 1941.
Alm, Ivar: Den religiösa funktionen i människosjälen. Stockholm: Diakonistyrelsens Förlag. 1936.
Ames, Edward Scribner: The Psychology of Religious Experience. Boston: Houghton Mifflin Company. 1910.
Asmussen, Hans: Die Seelsorge. München 1935.
Aubrey, Edwin Ewart: Man's Search for himself. Nashville: Cokesbury Press. 1940.
Augustine: St. Augustin's Confessions. English translation by William Watts. London: William Heineman. New York: O.P. Putnam's Sons. 1919.
Aulén, Gustaf: Dogmhistoria. Stockholm: Norstedt Bokförlag. 1933.
—, Den kristna Gudsbilden. Stockholm: Diakonistyrelsens Förlag. 1927.
Baille, John: Our nowledge of God. New York: Charles Scribner's Sons. 1939.
Berdyaev, Nicholas: Slavery and Freedom. New York: Charles Scribner's Sons. 1944.
—, The Destiny of Man. London: Goffrey Bless. 1948.
Berggrav, Eivind: Den religiöse fölelse i sundt sjeleliv. Oslo: Aschehoug. 1927.
—, Religionens terskel. Oslo: Aschehoug. 1924.
Bergman, Lorens: Kirkehistorie. København: J. Hasses Forlag. 1941.
Bergson, Henry: Den rene bevisshed. København: Gads Forlag. 1917.
Bergsten, Göte: Psykologi og sjelepleie. Oslo: Ansgar Forlag. 1946.
Bischof, Ledford J.: Interpreting Personality Theories. New York. Harper & Row. 1964.
Boisen, Anton T.: The Exploration of the inner World. Chicago: Willett, Clark, and Company. 1936.
—, Out of the Depths. New York: Harper and Brothers. 1960.
Bonnell, John Sutherland: Psychology for Pastor and Poeple. New York: Harper and Brothers. 1948.
Bonthius, Robert H.: Christian Paths to Self-Acceptance. New York: King's Crown Press. 1948.
Brown, William: Personality and Religion. London: University of London Press Ltd. 1946.
Brunner, Emil: The Christian Doctrine of God. Dogmatics Vol. I. Philadelphia: Westminster Press. 1950.
Bühler, Charlotte: Kindheit und Jugend. Leipzig: S. Hirzel. 1931.
—, Values in Psychotherapy. New York: The Free Press of Glencoe. 1962.
Buber, Martin: I and Thou. Edinburgh: T. and T. Clark. 1937.
Boehmer, Heinrich: Luther im Lichte der neueren Forschung. Leipzig und Berlin: Tuebner. 1917.
Cabot, R.C. and Dicks R.L.: The Art of Ministering to the Sick. New York: The Macmillan Co. 1936.
Calvin, John: Institutes. Edition of 1559.

Carrel, Alexis: Man, the Unknown. New York: Harper & Brothers. 1935.
Cameron, Norman: The Psychology of Behavior Disorders. Boston: Houghton Mifflin Co. 1947.
Cameron, Norman, and Ann, Margaret: Behavior Pathology. Boston: Houghton Mifflin Co. 1951.
Cannon, .B.: The Wisdom of the Body. New York: W.W. Norton Co. 1932.
Clark, Walter Houston: The Psychology of Religion. Toronto: The Macmillan Co. 1969.
Coe, George Albert: The Psychology of Religion. Chicago: The University of Chicago Press. 1916.
D:Arcy, M.C.: The Mind and Heart of Love. New York: Henry Holt & Co. 1947.
Davis, Henry. Moral and Pastoral Theology. New York: Shell and Ward. 1943.
Davis, W. Allison, and Havighurst, Robert Y.: Father of the Man. Boston: Houghton Mifflin Co. 1947.
Dick, Russel L.: Pastoral Work and Pastoral Counseling. New York: The Macmillan Co. 1944.
Dollard, John, and Miller, Nea E.: Personality and Psychotherapy. New York: Mc Graw and Hill Book Co. Inc. 1950.
Dunbar, Flanders: Psychosomatic Diagnosis. New York: Paul B. Hoeber, Inc. 1948.
English, O.S. and Pearson, G.H.: Emotional Problems of Living. New York: W.W. Norton. 1946.
Erikson, Erik H.: Childhood and Society. New York: W.W. Norton and Co. 1950.
—, Young Man Luther. New York: W.W. Norton and Co. 1958.
—, Identity, Youth, and Crisis. New York: W.W. Norton and Co. 1968.
Festinger, Leon: A Theory of Cognitive Dissonance. New York 1957.
Flanagan, J.C.: Factor Analysis in the Study of Personality. Palo Alto, California: Stanford University Press. 1935.
Flew, R. Newton: The Idea of Perfection in Christian Theology. London: Humphrey Milford, Oxford University Press. 1934.
Flewelling, R.T.: Creative Personality. New York: The Macmillan Co. 1926.
Fosdick, H.R.: The meaning of Prayer. New York: Association Press. 1938.
Frankl, Viktor Emil: The Doctor and the Soul. An Introduction to Logotherapy. Alfred A. Knopf, Inc. 1957.
—, Theorie und Therapie der Neurosen. Wien: Urban & Schwarzenberg. 1956.
—, Man's Search for Meaning. Boston: Beacon Press, 1959.
Freud, Sigmund: Totem und Tabu. Gesammelte Schriften. Band X. Leipzig: Psychoanalytischer Verlag. 1924.
Fromm, Erich: Escape from Freedom. New York: Farrar and Rinchart, 1941.
—, Psychoanalysis and Religion. New Haven: Yale University Press. 1950.
Fuglsang-Damgaard, H.: Religionspykologi. København. P. Haase & Søns Forlag. 1946.
Garrett, Henry E.: Great Experiments in Psychology. New York: D. Appleton-Century Co. 1930.
Girgensohn, E.: Der Seelische Aufbau der Religiösen Erlebensformen und ihre Psychologische Grundlage. Gütersloh: C. Bertelsmann. 1930.
Greeves, Frederik: Theology and the Cure of Souls. New York: Channel Press, Inc. 1962.
Gruehn, Werner: Das Werterlebnis. Leipzig: S. Hirtsel. 1924.
—, Die Frömmigkeit der Gegenwart. Münster/Westf.: Aschendorf. Archiev für Psychologie und Arbeit. 1956.
Grönbeck, Villiam: Om Beskrivelsen af Religiöse Oplevelser. Köbenhavn: Gads Forlag. 1935.
—, Religionspsykologi. Köbenhavn: Nyt Nordisk Forlag. 1958.
Hall, Calvin S., & Lindsey S.: Theories of Personality. New York: John Wileys and Sons. 1957.
Harper, Robert H.: Psychoanalysis and Psychotherapy. New York: Prentice Hall. Inc. 1965.
Harriman, Philip Lawrence: The Encyclopedia of Psychology. New York: Philosophical Library. 1945.
Hart, J.H. & Tomlinson, T.M.: New Directions in Clientcentered Therapy. New York: Houghton Mifflin Co. 1970.

Hiltner, Seward: Pastoral Counseling. New York: Abingdon Cokesbury Press. 1949.
Hofman, Hans: Making Ministry Relevant. New York: Charles Scribner's Sons. 1960.
—, Religion and Mental Health. New York: Harper and Brothers. 1961.
Hollingworth, H.L.: Psychology and Ethics. New York: The Donald Press. 1949.
Horney, Karen: The Neurotic Personality of our Time. New York: W.W. Norton and Co. Inc. 1937.
—, New Ways in Psychoanalysis. New York: W.W. Norton and Co. 1939.
—, Self Analysis. New York: W.W. Norton and Co. 1942.
—, Our Inner Conflicts. New York: W.W. Norton and Co. 1945.
Höffding, Harald: Oplevelse og Tydning. Köbenhavn: Nyt Nordisk Forlag. 1918.
James, William: The Energies of Man. New York: Moffatt, Yard and Co., 1911.
—, Varieties of Religious Experience. New York: Longmans, Green and Co. 1912.
Jung, C.G.: Modern Man in Search of a Soul. New York: Harcourt Brace. 1935.
—, The Integration of Personality. London: Kegan French, Trubner Co., Ltd. 1940.
—, Psychology of Religion. New Haven: Yale University Press. 1950.
—, The Practice of Psychotherapy. New York: Pantheon Books, Inc., 1954.
Kaila, Eino: Personlighetens Psykologi. Stockholm: Natur och Kultur. 1935.
Kirk, Kenneth E.: The Vision of God. London: Longmans, Green and Co. 1947.
Knudsen, Albert C.: The Doctrine of God. New York: Abingdon Press. 1930.
—, The Validity of Religious Experience. New York: Abingdon Cokesbury Press. 1937.
Källstad, Thorvald: John Wesley and the Bible. A Psychological Study. Acta Universitatis Upsaliensis, 1. Uppsala 1974.
Leuba, James H.: A Psychological Study of Religion. New York: The Macmillan Co. 1912.
Lecky, Prescott: Self-consistency: A Theory of Personality. New York: Island Press. 1945.
Lewin, Kurt: A Dynamic Theory of Personality. New York: McGraw-Hill Book Co., Inc. 1935.
Lindström, Harald: Wesley and Sanctification. London. Epworth Press. 1946.
Luria, A.R.: The Nature of Human Conflict. New York: Leveright. 1932.
Macintosch, D.C.: Theology as an Empirical Science. New York: The Macmillan Co. 1927.
Madsen, K.B.: Moderne psykologiske teorier. Köbenhavn: Munksgaard. 1967.
Maeder, A.: Veien til sjelelig sunnhet. Oslo: Land & Kirke. 1951.
Maslow, A.H.: Motivation and Personality. New York: Harper & Row. 1952.
—, New Knowledge in Human Values. Harper & Brothers. 1959.
May, Rollo: The Meaning of Anxiety. New York: The Ronald Press, Co. 1950.
—, Man's Search for Himself. New York: W.W. Norton Press. 1953.
May, Rollo, Angel, Ernest & Ellenberger, Henry F.: Existence: A New Dimension in Psychiatry and Psychology. New York: Basic Books. 1958.
Mead, George H.: Mind, Self, ans Society. Chicago: The University of Chicago Press. 1934.
McGiffert, A.C.: A History of Christian Thought. New York: Charles Scribner's Sons, Inc. 1932.
McKinney, F.: Psychology of Personal Adjustment. New York: John Wileys and Sons, Inc. 1941.
McNeill, John T.: A History of the Cure of Souls. New York: Harper and Brothers. 1951.
Menninger, Karl: Man against Himself. New York: Harcourt, Brace and Co. 1938.
—, Love against Hate. New York: Harcourt, Brace and Co. 1942.
Michalson, Carl: Faith for Personal Crises. New York: Charles Scribner's Sons. 1958.
Mowrer, O. Hobart: Learning Theory and Personality Dynamics. New York: The Ronald Press Co. 1950.
—, Psychotherapy: Theory and Research. New York: Ronald Press. 1953.
—, The Crisis in Psychiatry and Religion. New York: D. van Nostrand & Co. 1961.
Murphy, Gardner: Personality. New York: Harper and Brothers. 1947.
Nevius, Warren Nelson: Religion as Experience and Truth. Philadelphia: Westminster Press. 1941.

Niebuhr, Reinhold: The Nature and Destiny of man. New York: Charles Scribner's Sons 1941.
Nilsen, E. Anker: Nye veier i sjelesorgen. Oslo: Land & Kirke. 1957.
—, Kristenlivets kriser. Oslo: Norsk Forlagsselskap. 1958.
—, Personlige problemer. Oslo: Land & Kirke. 1960.
—, Pastoralrådgivning. Oslo: Luther Forlag. 1974.
Newman, Francis W.: The Soul, its Sorrows and its Aspirations. Third Edition 1852.
Nörregaard, Jens: Augustins Vej till Kristendommen. Köbenhavn: Jespersen & Pio Forlag. 1928.
Oates, Wayne E.: The Religious Dimensions of Personality. New York. Association Press. 1957.
—, An Introduction to Pastoral Counseling. Nashville: Broadman Press. 1959.
Oliver, J.R. Fear: The Autobiography of James Edwards. New York: The MacMillan Co. 1928.
Otto, Rudolf: The Idea od the Holy. London: Oxford University Press. 1943.
Petri, Laura: John Wesley. Stockholm: Nya Bokförlaget. 1929.
Plant, James S.: Personality and the Cultural Pattern. London: The Commonwealth Fund. Humphrey Milford. Oxford University Press. 1937.
Pratt, James Bisset: The Religious Consciousness. New York: The MacMillan Co. 1948.
Progoff, Ira: The Death aand Rebirth of Psychology. New York: The Julian Press, Inc. 1956.
Raknes, Ola: Møtet med det heilage. Oslo: Gyldendal. 1928.
Rogers, Carl R.: Counseling and Psychotherapy. Boston: Houghton Mifflin Co. 1942.
—, Clientcentered Therapy. Boston: Houghton Mifflin Co. 1951.
—, On Becoming a Person. Boston: Houghton Mifflin Co. 1961.
Rommetveit, Ragnar: Ego i moderne psykologi. Oslo: Universitetsforlaget. 1958.
Schjelderup, Harald: Neuroserna och den neurotiska karaktären. Stockholm: Natur och Kultur. 1940.
Schjelderup, Harald und Kristian: Über drei Haupttypen der religiösen Erlebnisformen und ihre psychologische Grundlage. Berlin: de Gruiter. Oslo Cammermeyer. 1932.
Schleiermacher, Friedrich: The Christian Faith. Edinburgh: T. & T. Clark. 1928.
Schweitzer, Albert: The Philosophy of Civilization. New York: The MacMillan Co. 1950.
Söderblom, Nathan: Studier Övfer Gudstrons Uppkomst. Stockholm: Geber Förlag. 1914.
Stagner, Ross: Psychology of Personality. New York: McGraw-Hill Co. Inc. 1937.
Starbuck, E.D.: The Psychology of Religion. London: W. Scott. New York: C. Scribner's Sons. 1901.
Stewart, James S.: A Man in Christ. New York: Harper and Brothers.
Stolz, Karl Ruf: The Church and Psychotherapy. New York: Abingdon-Cokesbury Press 1943.
Sundén, Hjalmar: Religionen och rollerna. Stockholm: Diakonistyrelsens Bokförlag. 1959.
Symonds, Percival M.: Dynamic Psychology. New York: Appleton-Century-Crofts, Inc. 1949.
—, The Ego and the Self. New York: Appleton-Century-Crofts, Inc. 1951.
Thorndike, E.L.: Psychology of Wants, Interests, and Attitudes. New York: D. Appleton-Century Co., Inc. 1935.
Thurneysen, Eduard: Die Lehre von der Seelsorge. Zürich: Evangelischer Verlag. 1957.
Tillich, Paul: The Courage to be. New Haven: Yale University Press. 1952.
—, Systematic Theology. Vol. I. Chicago: The University of Chicago Press. 1959.
Tweedie, Donald F.: Logotherapy and the Christian Faith. Mich: Baker Book House. 1961.
Ungersma, A.J.: The Search for Meaning. Philadelphia: The Westminster Press. 1961.
Vulliamy, C.E.: John Wesley. New York: Charles Scribner's Sons. 1932.
Wieman, Henry Nelson: The Source of Human Good. Chicago: The University of Chicago Press. 1946.
Werner, Heinz: Einführung in die Entwicklungspsychologie. Leipzig: Joh-Ambr. Barth. 1926.

Wesley, John: The Journal of John Wesley. London: J.M. Dent & Sons, Ltd., New York: E.P. Dutton & Co. Inc. 1930.
—, The Journal of John Wesley. A. M. ed. by Nehemiah Curnock. New York: Eaton and Mains. 1916.
Wise, Carrol A.: Religion in Illness and Health. New York: Harper and Brothers. 1942. Pastoral Counseling. New York: Harper and Brothers. 1951.
—, Psychiatry and the Bible. New York: Harper and Brothers. 1956.
Wobbermin, Georg: Systematische Theologie nach religions-psychologischer Methode. Leipzig: J.C. Henrichs. 1925.
Young, Kimbal: Personality and Problems of Adjustment. New York: F.S. Crofts & Co. 1940.
Young, Paul Thomas: Emotions in Man and Animal. New York: John Wiley & Sons, Inc. 1943.